MW01178281

SO FAR-
SO GOOD

AN AUTOBIOGRAPHY

BY

BERNARD WILKINSON BRAITHWAITE

Grosvenor House
Publishing Limited

This book is published by
Grosvenor House Publishing Ltd
28-30 High Street, Guildford, Surrey, GU1 3EL.
www.grosvenorhousepublishing.co.uk

A CIP record for this book
is available from the British Library

ISBN 978-1-78148-986-4

CHAPTER ONE

The following may be apocryphal, although there could just *as* well be some truth in it, but it is said that shortly before my mother was delivered of her baby she was talking to a friend on the corner of Pickering's the chemist when she was asked by a policeman to "move along there please" because she was blocking the progress of other shoppers, being so very large. This was long before scans were available to determine the contents of the womb and although mother believed she was carrying twins this was not confirmed until the actual event on the 4th March 1923. Two of my aunts were in attendance. My twin brother was the first to show his face to the world and I followed shortly after. Both my aunts claim the dubious privilege of nursing me back to life and it doesn't now matter which of them it was but I am glad it was one of them. Although brother Derek claims to be older than me by some minutes I have read that the first twin to be conceived is the last to be delivered but, again, it doesn't really matter. The accuracy or otherwise of the story about the policeman is borne out to some degree by the fact that both of us were in excess of 7 pounds birth weight. The picture shows us at 7 days old and speaks for itself.

Fortunately we can skip over the first few years of my life for I cannot remember much about it. My parents at that time could afford to employ a maid and another picture shows me with one at a later age. I often wonder if childhood memories are not real memories but recollections of stories told to us by our parents of what we got up to as small children. There is a story told that, and this is at a time when motor cars were a fairly rare sight on our roads, that I sat brother Derek in the middle of the road and almost covered him with leaves. Fortunately a motorist did see him and was able to stop in time so all was well. Yet another story tells how I went across the road to the house of Mr. and Mrs. Murray – he had a shoe shop in the town – and pleaded hunger because my parents did not give me enough to eat. Surely these must be more apocryphal than the one about my mother. Yet another story concerns me being reprimanded by a maid for killing a spider. She asked me what the spider's mother would think, my reply being, "it's alright I killed its mother yesterday".

My very first actual memory was of a mask being placed over my face. As well as births being carried out at home,

Here is a picture of Derek and me (I am on the left) climbing on the fence of the house in Etherley Lane showing how adventurous we were at an early age. In any picture of the two of us Derek was always the larger boy.

minor operations were also done on the kitchen table and this was the occasion of the removal of my tonsils.

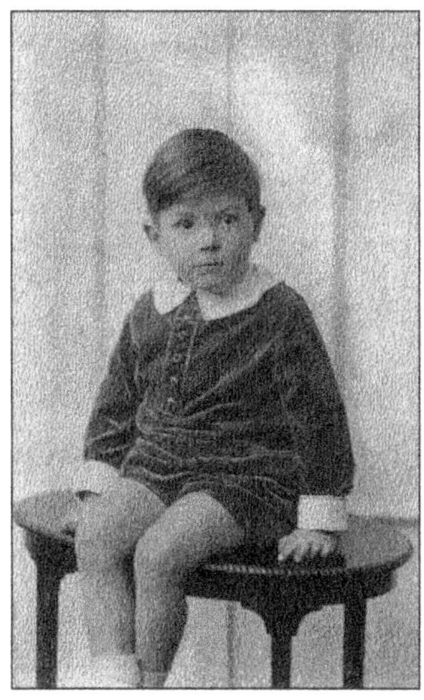

And here I am, growing a little older and dressed in my best velvet suit.

Our first shopping expeditions were to a little shop, created out of a cottage in the middle of a row some 50 yards along the road from our house, which was run by Mrs. Chisholm. To us it was an Aladdin's cave of sweets in rows of jars on shelves behind the counter. I am sure Mrs. Chisholm got tired of our visits but we never did.

The house in which we spent about the first five years of our lives was a semi-detached stone built house called "Ashville" in Etherley Lane, Bishop Auckland which was still standing in 1985 when we paid a nostalgic visit to the North of England in that year.

Further along Etherley Lane was the manse occupied by a Methodist minister, the incumbent at about this time being Rev. Bertram Dewhirst, who had a daughter Jean, about whom more anon.

Apart from a short time spent at a kindergarten in the market place all my formal education was at Cockton Hill council school, firstly the Infant's and then the Boy's school. By that time the family had moved to Newlands Avenue in the Cockton Hill part of the town, presumably to make it easier for elder brother Jack and we twins to get to school. I hated it. On the first day I was to drag there from my position with my arms entwined round a lamp-post to prevent further progress. I lost, but with an ill grace and loud wailing. I think I had made up my mind from an early date that school was not for me and I suppose this was the first of many mistakes I have made in my life.

In the Infants school boys and girls were in the same class and, although it may sound strange, the first writing instruments I used were a slate and a slate pencil. Whatever had been written on the slate could easily be removed with a bit of cloth and a bit of spit so, in a sense, it was an early word processor. I can recall the teacher doing cursive writing on the blackboard, which we had to copy letter by letter. The last class in the Infants was presided over by Miss Connie Ireland who did nothing to change my opinion of school.

During my early school years I suffered from a skin disease on one or other, and sometimes both, of my hands, which required the application of bandages. Corporal punishment was available to teachers and often used to good effect. When my hands were bandaged Miss Ireland used her strap on my bare legs. One of the methods of trying to cure my skin disease was the application of a bread poultice. This involved making a mash of bread and water spread on medical gauze, heated over a stove, and applied to the affected area. I have never taken bread sauce from that day and people wonder why.

The Girls and the Infants were located on one side of a line of iron railings with spikes on top with the Boys on the other side. Elevation to the Boys school was to cross the divide. The Boys school had alongside it an area of open ground which was all right for football, not much good for cricket, but ideal for marbles. With our fingers we would scoop out soil to make small saucer like depressions and shoot our glass alleys (marbles) to try and get them to land in these. Once a year the traveling fair took up residence in the field beside the school which was a cause for great jubilation and a general reduction in our attention to schoolwork as we could see from our classroom windows fairground rides being assembled.

My interest in learning remained at a low ebb and while both my brothers obtained scholarships to the Grammar School I spent the rest of my school days at Cockton Hill taking as little interest as possible in its activities apart, that was, from mid-morning and mid-afternoon breaks, known as play-time, and the girls on the other side of the railings.

One of the teachers, Mr. Elland, was very adept at punishment, administering to those who had displeased him what he referred to as his 'Napoleon', so named because he aimed his cane at the 'bony-part' of the hand at the base of the thumb and by Jove didn't it sting. Apart from that he was quite a nice man who used to teach English and Music. Can you picture a class of 50 fourteen-year-old boys singing 'It was a lover and his lass'?.

Outside the school gates as we left there stood a roguish looking old Italian called Luigi with his bicycle ice cream cart. On the odd occasion when we had a penny we would get an ice cream cornet from him and ask that it be adorned with what we referred to as 'monkey blood'. This was a sort of red juice or syrup which enhanced our enjoyment of this rare treat.

School days were never the happiest days of my life and I was quite glad when they were over. Thinking back I regret that it was not otherwise and life might have been very different if I had taken advantage of more learning, who knows.

We had moved from Etherley Lane to 35 Newlands Avenue which was the end house in a street lined with lime trees. The houses were almost all 3/4 bedroom semi-detached with small gardens back and front. In our back garden was a tall silver birch tree which was wonderful for climbing and I'm sure mother must have been worried at the heights to which we used to climb. There were fireplaces in all but the smaller rooms (no central heating) and a large kitchen fireplace with ovens and a back-boiler to heat the water. What is now referred to as a utility room was then known as a scullery, off which was a pantry (the equivalent of today's fridge). Of course a coalhouse was needed and this was outside. We did have a gas fire in one living room.

My best friend of those days, Laurie Crawford, lived a few doors down on the other side of the street and I can still recall the names of many of the street's residents. Beyond the end of the street were fields belonging to Blackett's farm. One of them contained a pond where we caught newts and frogspawn and in the corner of that same field were tennis courts owned by the Methodist Church which played a part in later life.

Outside number 35 was a lamp-post (not the one I had clung to on my first school day). These were lit by gas and every evening the lamp lighter would come round with his long pole at the end of which was some sort of flame. He would stick the pole up into the glass box at the top, push a lever to turn the gas on, and wait for the gas to light. The following morning he came round and turned the gas off again.

It was possible for an agile, and naughty, lad to shin (climb) up the lamppost and turn the lever off to plunge the area into darkness. I can vouch for this but do not now think it was a very sensible thing to do. I tended to get myself into trouble over pranks like this and I am sure there were many times my parents must have despaired of me and what I would become. While my studious brothers were slogging over homework I was out playing.

During all my time in Bishop Auckland the Methodist church played a significant part in my life. The church was an outstanding feature of the main street of the town, built of stone with a tall square clock tower. My great grandfather had been one of the leading lights in it's building and there was a plaque inside the church to this effect. Sadly, it is now closed as a church but has become a community centre.

First, at a very early age, was Sunday School both morning and afternoon presided over by Mr. Ferens who was later to give me a wedding present of an EPNS teapot and water jug. When we started to be taken to actual church services we were excused morning Sunday School. Because, I suppose, we three boys were a bit of a handful for mother we occupied the very back pew under the gallery. At the time when Mr. Dewhirst was a minister the pew some five places in front was occupied by Mrs. Dewhirst and her daughter Jean (again of whom more anon).

My paternal grandfather was a steward and I remember before each service began he would open the vestry door and peer down the length of the church to see what sort of a congregation had gathered. Father was the regular organist so he seldom sat with us but we could see him at work behind the choir stalls. He was also the custodian of the church clock, climbing up into the tower to wind, regulate, or alter the time when summer time came along. Mother, and the influence of the church, gave us a puritan up-bringing, never actually at any time telling us the 'facts of life' but warning us against all sorts of evils we might meet in life.

Amongst the congregation were The Superintendent of Police, his wife and their two daughters. We were very friendly with them and often played tennis with the daughters, Dorothy and Joan, at the aforementioned tennis courts. Brother Jack subsequently married Dorothy.

CHAPTER TWO

When I was due to leave school shortly after my fourteenth birthday with no educational qualifications it became necessary for my parents to decide what I should do. I do not recall having any say in the matter.

M. Braithwaite & Son, Printers, Stationers & Booksellers shop on the corner of the Market Place and Newgate Street in Bishop Auckland

Father was the fourth generation owner of a stationers, booksellers and printers business. He was originally destined to be an electrical engineer but his brother Jack having been killed in the First World War, his family expected him to carry on the family business for which he had had no training. His father, my grandfather, had died during my school days.

From a school day of some 6 hours a day 5 days a week with long holidays I was pitched into the family printing works as an apprentice with a working week of 60 hours and a weekly wage of 12 shillings (60 pence). I cycled to work for 8 a.m., back home again at 12 noon for dinner (a midday meal in those days) then back to work at 1 o'clock until 6 p.m. for five weekdays and on Saturday from 8 a.m. to 1 p.m. The printing side of the business had been neglected, as father had no training in it so, inevitably, it declined but not necessarily just because I had joined it. I joined 4 men in the printing department and one man and several girls in the binding department. The original central heating had packed in long before I got there and it was so cold in the winter with only a small fire in each department to try and keep warm by. In spite of the very big change from school I did enjoy work much more than I had enjoyed lessons. It was heavy work setting small pieces of lead type into a hand held 'stick' and then transferring the 'stickful' onto a 'galley' where the lines of type were made up into pages. Lead pieces were used where necessary to separate the lines of type so by the end the finished page or pages were pretty heavy. When these were locked into a 'chase' or steel frame with metal 'furniture' the weight was greatly increased.

The 'chase' then had to be taken downstairs to the appropriate printing machine or 'press' where it was locked into place before the printing began. The bigger machines were operated by a belt from an electric motor but the smaller ones on which handbills, stationery and the like were manually operated by a foot treadle. Much of my early days were spent standing on one foot and pedaling away with the other one on a platen machine and at the same time taking the printed sheet out of the machine and placing a blank sheet in it – very quickly or ones fingers would get caught in the machine.

Washing up a machine was the worst job. With cotton waste soaked in paraffin the rollers and the ink slab had to be rubbed down to remove all traces of the ink which, if left, would dry on the rollers and ruin them. Trying to then wash ones hands in cold water did not do much to get the ink off.

It would have been 1937 when I went to work so 2 years later the Second World War came along when I would have been 16 1/2 years old.

Father had formed a scout troop some time earlier and, of course, we three boys were all members of it. Our first meeting place was the church hall and sometime later we moved to the cellar of a relation of the Assistant Scout Master, which sounds a bit grim but was really quite good. As scouts we were roped in to be part of the A.R.P. (Air raid precautions) organization and became messengers at the H.Q. in the basement of the town hall. When the air raid siren was sounded we would don our tin hats and cycle down to the town hall ready to risk life and limb to take messages wherever. Fortunately there was never much risk as Bishop Auckland suffered no attentions from the Luftwaffe.

As the time came near that I was old enough to be called up I decided that the armed forces were not for me. I did not fancy being posted to some god-forsaken place for maybe years on end as some soldiers were. Instead I had a hankering to go off to sea and where I got that from I do not know. However it turned out to be one of my better decisions. I discovered there was a radio school in Newcastle which did short courses in radio telegraphy and if one could obtain a special wartime certificate of proficiency one could go to sea in the Merchant Navy as a Radio Officer and this is what I did.

Catching an early morning bus from the market place for the hour-long journey to Newcastle I then took a tram to near where the school was and spent the day there, doing the reverse journey in the late afternoon. As a result of this I discovered that if I really wanted something I *was* prepared to work for it. Work I did, obtaining my certificate at the first try. The next thing was to apply to the Marconi Marine Radio Company for a job which was not too difficult as they were crying out for radio officers for merchant ships. Where previously most ships, and particularly the smaller ones, carried only one radio officer they now had to carry 3 so that a continuous radio watch could be kept. So, I was all ready to sail off into the sunset, but it was not to be – not just yet anyway.

At this same time the owners of the radio school had an appeal for radio operators to fly with, but not to join, the Royal Air Force. This was an opportunity not to be missed so I jumped at it and found myself bound for Ansty aerodrome just outside Coventry. This was a private, or public if you like, airfield which had been taken over by the R.A.F. to train observers. The R.A.F. supplied the aeroplanes (twin engine Avro Anson's), the pilots, and the trainee observers, but for some strange reason not the radio operators. I found accommodation some distance away with a family in Hinckley so transport was a problem and I solved this by purchasing a second hand motor bike which served me well for that period and enabled me to drive home on occasions. It was there I had probably the narrowest squeak of my life. Having been accustomed, in Bishop Auckland, to ignoring an air raid warning I did so in Hinckley and was still in bed when a German incendiary bomb came through the roof of the house and lodged in the ceiling of my room right above my bed. Had it not stuck where it did I might not be telling the tale now.

Most of our flights were of about two hours duration and more often than not took us into Wales, or along the north Wales coast where we would zoom along the beach at Rhyl at a very low level, do a little hop over the pier then down again before coming up before we got to Llandudno. Other times we flew over the Irish Sea to the Isle of Man which I had only seen from the air (at that time).. The flying was good fun until several things happened. It was at this time I heard that brother Jack had been shot down over Germany in his bomber which unsettled me about flying; I was, as the youngest radio operator, saddled with quite a lot of extra and late flying; I was becoming increasingly air sick; and I still hankered after going to sea. I stuck the flying for several months but decided it was not for me so gave it up and headed for the wide oceans.

CHAPTER THREE

Marconi's were only too glad to have me and very soon I was to be found in their office in Newcastle-upon-Tyne awaiting instructions to join a ship. It was with both delight and in trepidation, now the moment had arrived, that I found myself mounting the gangway of the M.V. Empire Flint, a tanker of some 12,000 tons, at Wallsend where she had recently been built and launched and was about to set out on her maiden voyage. For some reason ships were always feminine. I had met my two senior colleagues at the Marconi office but had to face, as a very raw recruit, the rest of what were probably seasoned officers. I cannot recall there being any problems about this and I very soon settled into ship-board ways and nautical language. Companionways instead of stairs; alleyways instead of corridors; decks instead of floors; portholes instead of windows and so on. As we sailed down the river Tyne towards the sea suddenly all hell was let loose and I heard nearby gunfire and further off crumps. An air raid was in progress and some of the ship's armament had been pressed into use. What an introduction, I thought, and wondered what I had let myself in for. We reached the sea and sailed north round the top of Scotland to the Clyde where ships assembled to join an outward bound convoy and there we waited for our eventual departure.

In passing, and in connection with Scotland, I recall two very typical deeds of kindness by Scots folk which I never forget. One time when in Glasgow I went into the restaurant of a department store to have some lunch. It was busy and I joined a table with an older couple half way through their meal. We got to talking a little and presently they took their leave. When it came to my turn to leave and to pay I was told the couple had paid my bill for me. On another occasion I had been home to Bishop Auckland on leave and returned to Glasgow quite late at night where I had to take another train to Gourock where the ship was anchored mid-stream in the Clyde. At Glasgow station I was in a compartment on my own, in the blackout, when the carriage door was opened and a lady shone a torch into it to see who might be there. She must have thought I would be a safe companion for she got in and, again, we did a little talking. She was also bound for Gourock where she lived and when I told her I was hoping to join a ship at anchor she assured me there would be no boats to take me out to the ship. Whereupon she invited me to spend the night at her house, with her family, which I gladly did and shared their breakfast next morning. Wartime often tended to bring out the best in some folk and I was fortunate to meet quite a lot of them.

Eventually there were enough ships to warrant a convoy with Royal Navy warships as escorts and we sailed for New York. In 1941/42 the Navy escorted convoys for 3 or 4 days only and then sent them all off on their own to their various destinations. This was before the German submarines were able to travel further afield. The average time for a merchant ship to cross the Atlantic was about 14 days. We kept radio watch for 4 hours on and 8 hours off, as did the navigation officers on the bridge and the engineer officers down in the engine room. The food was very good, far better than was available to those at home with rationing to cope with and we really lived very well. On this ship I had a fair sized cabin to myself complete with washbasin.

The North Atlantic Ocean is one of the roughest seas in the world. The plimsoll line on the side of a ship indicates the level below which she should not be loaded. Below the normal plimsoll line is another line marked WNA which stands for Winter North Atlantic to allow more leeway for a possible very rough passage. Tankers lie very low in the water at the best of times and I have to admit I was a little scared as the ship rolled until the deck at each side was under the water by turn but one soon got used to it and, anyway, there was nothing I could do about it. The fury of the North Atlantic at its worst has to really be experienced to be believed.

We arrived in the Narrows, the entrance to New York harbour, early one morning and I remember staying up on deck hoping to see skyscrapers. When they did emerge from the early morning mist they were still a long way away but nevertheless quite impressive. Almost every city has them now but 60 years ago it was very different. We docked at New Jersey which is the other side of the bay to New York to which there were constant ferries, as there are to this day, buzzing about the harbour to wherever and we were able to get shore leave and head for the big apple. I am not now sure how I came to get a ticket to attend a ball in the Waldorf Astoria Hotel on Times Square but attend I did and, once again, met up with a hospitable family from Long Island. Perhaps it was because they had two pretty daughters that drew me in their direction so I had a wonderful time, probably treading on the girl's feet as I tried to dance with them. The family invited me to visit them which I gladly did and also on several other occasions when my ship called in at New York. It was wonderful to see lights again after two years of blackout in the U.K. The trip up the Empire State building was quite something, as was a visit to a show at the Rockefeller Centre.

Meanwhile the ship was being loaded with 10,000 tons of high octane aviation fuel to keep the R.A.F. flying. The merest spark would be disastrous and a torpedo would have turned the ship into a fireball. Any tools used about the deck were made of brass rather than steel to avoid the possibility of a spark. Although on a lot of the outward journey we sailed independently the homeward journey was in convoy the whole way. The assembly point for these was Halifax in Nova Scotia which had a wonderful harbour and there cannot be many merchant seamen who have not experienced the delights of an eating place called The Green Lantern where I first came across that new world dish – pie a la mode – along with other non rationed delights. Most convoys were of anything from 60 to 100 ships which took up a lot of ocean. They were nearly always wider than they were from back to front with as many as twelve columns broad and 8 or 9 ships following each other in each column. The convoy commodore was in the central leading ship from which emanated all sorts of messages either by flag hoists or by aldis lamp signals. More often than not when we were in convoy the radio officers stood a bridge watch rather than a radio watch so we could read Morse code signals from the commodore. The return journey was almost always slower because the convoy had to keep to the speed of the slowest ship. For the faster, mainly passenger liners, there were speedier convoys.

Whilst I no longer have a record of all the ships I was in during my 5 years at sea, nor a clear recollection of all the journeys I made, naturally some things stand out and you must be content with what I can recall of an interesting nature.

In the M.V. Empire Flint I made six crossings of the Atlantic in six months. The second trip was to the Dutch West Indies colony of Aruba, again to collect aviation spirit. This trip gave me my first experience of wonderful, balmy tropic days and nights in the Caribbean Sea. Having loaded our cargo we sailed independently up the East coast of the U.S.A. to Halifax to join a homeward bound convoy. Tankers were able to load and unload their cargo much more speedily than dry cargo ships so we were seldom in port for more than a few days. The return port on this occasion was Belfast where we spent Christmas Eve, Christmas Day and Boxing Day. It was impossible to find a pub that you could get into, they were all crowded, or a cinema with any vacant seats, or a dance hall with room for any more and in the end I had to make do with a visit to the hospital. Shortly after we had left Halifax I developed a nosebleed which I could not stop. For most of the 14 days we sailed home I had one nostril stuffed with cotton wool and a plaster. The hospital cauterized it for me which lasted for some time. When it happened again we were in Canada and again I had the nose cauterized. When it happened a third time we were on our way to the Panama Canal and an American doctor operated on it at a hospital in Cristobal and inserted a number of stitches. When I returned to the ship with a bright red nose and swathed in bandages I suffered some ribbing from my colleagues.

Although on each ship the radio officers were signed on as part of the crew they were usually signed off again at the end of a voyage to take any leave which had become due, so I signed off the Empire Flint, after three trips, at the port of Liverpool. Railway journeys during wartime were pretty grim and I can recall on another occasion landing at Liverpool at a bank holiday week-end which gave the opportunity of a short week-end at home before the ship signed off. I travelled by train from Liverpool to Darlington on Thursday, from Darlington to Liverpool on the Tuesday, and Liverpool to Darlington again on the Wednesday (after signing off) and stood all the way on all three journeys – with a First Class Ticket. In the blackout you had to be careful to see you had got to the correct station and to make sure the train really was standing at the platform and that you got out at the correct side.

Having had what leave was due we had to return to the Marconi office at the port where we had previously landed so, for me, it was back to Liverpool to see what awaited me. Shipping lines were identified by the colour or colours on their funnels and the line I joined on this occasion had a black funnel with a thin red stripe with a larger white stripe above and below it. This was a ship of the T. and J. Harrison

Line whose ships were all named after occupations and this one was the S.S. Rancher. From the marks on their funnels they were familiarly known as 'two of fat and one of lean' being an indication of their record of providing poor food. Having gone from a new clean ship I had landed an old bucket alive with cockroaches and rats. This was a coal burning steam ship and the residue of coal dust after a refueling seemed to permeate everywhere. The captain was rather deaf and failed to hear all the instructions given to the captain of each ship at a pre-sailing convoy conference so we more or less followed my leader. We did manage to make it to New Orleans but only just. The ship could muster some 10 knots of speed but the mighty Mississippi river flowed downstream at the rate of about 8 knots so it was a hard pull upstream to New Orleans. Many ports had clubs of one sort or another for sailors and New Orleans was one of them. I remember distinctly being told about a 'cat club' which 13 of the girls who attended the club had organized amongst themselves. Twelve of them met once a month and spent the meeting talking about number 13. It cannot have been much fun in the month when you were the one left out. So it was back to Halifax once again. On the return convoy we met the worst storm I ever experienced. It was impossible for ships to keep station on one another as they were being tossed about like the proverbial corks. The convoy was ordered to scatter with every ship proceeding independently. It had been my understanding that submarines could not operate in such stormy seas but through the night we received distress signals from at least 3 ships nearby reporting having been torpedoed. I fear there was not much hope for any of them in those conditions but we eventually made it back to the U.K. safe and sound.

The Pacific Steamship Navigation Company traded up and down the West coast of South America and on the S.S. Loriga we headed in that direction, first of all making a call in Havana in Cuba about which I do not remember much.

An enterprising photographer in Havana must have been in the habit of photographing incoming vessels in the hope of selling copies to crew members.

This trip took us for the first of my five passages through the Panama Canal which was quite an experience. We called at Callao, the port for the city of Lima, in Peru. There was a pretty fast tram ride from the port to the city and the travellers, nearly all of whom would be Catholics, rapidly crossed themselves as the tram sped past the many churches along or beside the line. Other stops for discharging our cargo of general goods were at Mollendo (pronounced Moyendo): Iquique (pronounced Eyekeykey): Arica: Antofagasta, and other small unpronounceable places before arriving at Valparaiso which was as far south as we went. The return journey was back through the canal and inevitably to Halifax for the convoy across the Atlantic. Nearly all my journeys were across the Atlantic but not quite all as you will see.

Another trip to the West Indies and the Caribbean was on the M.V. Tetela a ship of the banana firm, Elders and Fyffe's. The cargo was not bananas on this occasion, they were hardly ever seen in war-time Britain and many children never saw a banana until the war was over. We collected a cargo of meat which went into the refrigerated holds. These ships are notorious for their cuisine and I can vouch for it. I do not think I have ever had such a long spell of imaginative and interesting meals as I had on the Tetela and I could not help feeling sorry for the folks at home on their meagre rations whilst I was living it up. They also had accommodation for about 12 passengers and I remember, I would, wouldn't I, one of them was the Honourable Shirley Cunliffe. I think that was the only time I have ever rubbed shoulders with the nobility.

I sailed in two ship of the New Zealand Shipping Company. Firstly on the M.V. Taranaki across the Atlantic and through the Panama Canal again for a 28 day journey from Colon at the end of the Canal to Sydney in Australia For that 28 days the only other thing we saw, apart from the sea and flying fish, was the flashing light from the lighthouse on the northern tip of New Zealand as we sailed by at night. This ship carried 6 passengers who came aboard at New York where we called on our way. Three of them were American missionaries going eventually to China, India and Africa. One I forget, but the other two were a sergeant of the Australian police who was escorting back to Australia a Woolcott Forbes who was a famous, or infamous perhaps, financial swindler. He had been caught in the U.S.A. trying to swindle some old lady out of a fortune and was headed back for trial in Australia. Just a few hours after we had docked in Sydney harbour the local radio announced that "Woolcott Forbes is back in Australia". I wonder what his fate was. Although we met with the passengers on deck and at meal times we did not mix with them in their accommodation but were told that Mr. Forbes and the 3 missionaries played quite a lot of Monopoly and that the swindler almost always won!

There was an active seaman's mission in Sydney with pleasant friendly girls and on one occasion a group of us were taken on an outing and picnic somewhere down the coast. It was very enjoyable to be entertained in this way in a strange place by nice people and the hospitality I experienced in so many places added a bonus to what was, most of the time, quite a good life far away from the problems of people in wartime Britain. Along with one of the deck officers I attended a dance in Sydney town hall together with a couple of Australian W.A.A.A.F.s.

From Sydney we sailed to Port Chalmers, the port for Dunedin in the South Island of New Zealand. This was sheep country and it was frozen carcasses of sheep that we loaded into the ship's holds by the ton to help boost the meagre meat rations of the folks back home.

The journey back across the Pacific Ocean was not quite so long from this starting point. It is a little known fact that the Panama Canal which takes ships from the East side of Central America to the West side actually runs from West to East. By this time German submarines were able to operate close to the east coast of America so there were now convoys along that coast to Halifax before the journey back to the U.K.

CHAPTER FOUR

The S.S. Baltrover was a small passenger ship belonging to the Baltic Steam Shipping Company which, in peace-time had plied the Baltic Sea. Returning to the Marconi office in Newcastle-upon-Tyne from leave and crossing the bridge over the River Tyne in a bus I saw this small ship alongside the quay under the bridge and wondered what it was. Later that day I was climbing it's gangway and making my way aboard my latest temporary home. Strangely, I cannot recall which passengers, if any, we took on the outward journey. These were now in convoy all the way and usually sailed from an assembly anchorage in Loch Ewe in Scotland. The destination was, would you believe, Halifax where we took aboard women and children who had been evacuated, at the beginning of the war, to Canada and who now wished to return. Some of the women coming aboard such a small ship for a journey over the Atlantic thought it was the tender which was transferring them to the large passenger liner they had obviously hoped for. Half way across the ship broke down with engine trouble and the convoy slowed down to keep us with them for a while. We could not make the necessary speed which was required so it was decided the convoy should proceed and we were left to make our own way home as best we could. A destroyer of the convoy escort came alongside and explained what was to happen and then zoomed off at the rate of knots to rejoin the convoy now far ahead. We did get all our passengers safely home, I suspect more by good luck than good management

The second ship of the New Zealand Shipping Company which I joined was the Moreton Bay, a sister ship of the famous Jarvis Bay which was an ill fated armed merchant liner in an encounter with a German Battleship. This trip was to New York in a fast convoy.

In New York it was good to meet up again with the Long Island family and their blonde daughter Lynn. Their other older daughter had, by this time, met and married an R.A.F. officer. America was now on our side in the war fighting the Germans. Accommodation for troops had been built in the upper holds of the Moreton Bay and there was accommodation for officers in passenger cabins so we loaded crowds of G.I's. and their officers for an uneventful trip back to the U.K. The Americans required a safety check on the ship so we had a lifeboat drill while alongside the quay in the Hudson River. On our trip home we had extra duties in the radio room as the radio frequency of the Americans was not the same as the British so we operated equipment to translate the one into the other. On this, as on most ships, we were in charge of the 'domestic' radio and ensured that broadcasts of news and entertainment programmes were sent to the crew's mess decks and the officer's saloon.

Arriving at the Newcastle office of Marconi, after leave, I was given the option of joining a ship which was bound for Murmansk in Russia or of going to Vancouver to join a new ship being built there. Russian convoys were notorious for hardship and the level of ship losses so I decided to let fate decide for me and said I would join whichever ship was being signed on first. Fortunately it turned out to be the Canadian one. The whole crew was signed on in Newcastle to a ship which was still being completed in a Vancouver shipyard. We went by train to the Clyde where we boarded the P. & O. cruise liner Andes. Cruising days had finished and in a cabin originally designed for one or two people there were nine of us. Our destination was Halifax where our ship's crew boarded a train for Montreal for a few days' stay in a hotel there. Then aboard another train for the 6 day journey across Canada. This was winter-time so much of the scenery was covered in snow and when we got off the train at various stops to stretch our legs it was mighty cold. We fed in a dining car and while we took our evening meal the attendant made up our beds, one on the two facing seats pulled together and the other pulled down from the roof. They were very comfortable with clean linen every night and the motion of the train to quickly send us to sleep. What a remarkable feat of engineering was the railway line along the Fraser River and what wonderful scenery as we approached Vancouver where, again, we were housed in a hotel but without a restaurant. We ate in a smallish café further down the road. We had a few weeks before the ship was ready for us so it was more like a holiday than anything else. One evening some of us went roller- skating and I met Pat Wylie with whom I had some good times. I also earned some money by working for the Canadian National Railways as a wagon loader. I can recall loading a freight car with boxes of fruit for delivery to Kamloops. The ship, when we joined her, turned out to be the S.S. Fort Stager. It was one of a number of specially produced wartime vessels all named after the old Canadian forts. We sailed across to Vancouver Island to Nanaimo where we loaded timber. A lady there told my fortune and said I would make an invention, which I am still waiting to make! Then down the west coast of America for my fifth trip through the Panama Canal and home by the usual routine.

Shortly after the allies crossed the English Channel to invade France I joined another Vancouver built ship. the S.S. Fort St. Paul, in the Thames. We became part of the fleet of merchant ships ferrying men and supplies to the Normandy beaches in support of our troops battling against the German army. I cannot remember how many trips we made from the Thames to the beachhead but it was quite a few, some more dicey than others. We always passed through the Straits of Dover at night time because the Germans still had long-range guns on the French coast. It was usually a noisy passage nevertheless with German E-boats dodging about, British Motor Torpedo boats trying to catch them, guns from both the British and French sides and German V 1 flying bombs thundering above us. There were ships torpedoed and it was distressing to hear voices from the water crying for help which we were not allowed to stop to give.

The Mulberry harbour created at the Arromanches beach was a wonderful feat of engineering. We carried personnel and all manner of vehicles which had to be lifted in and out of the holds in cradles mostly onto motor barges tied up alongside the ship for the short journey to the shore.

Most of the loading was done at Tilbury docks, which lie over the Thames from Gravesend where I spent any spare time and where I met a family who were so kind and hospitable. Fortunately they had three daughters and I enjoyed visits to the cinema and some enjoyable cycle rides in the pleasant Kent countryside with Mary. I never kept in touch with any of the girls I met in various places but I have happy memories of their friendship.

On one of our journeys up or down the Thames we were in collision with an Isle of Man paddle steamer, the Ben-my-Chree. We nearly sliced her in half while our bow was pushed back by about 15 feet. For repairs the ship was sent to Antwerp in Belgium which had recently been re-captured from the Germans who were still not very far away. We went into dry dock which meant the ship was resting on its keel and propped against the side of the dock with huge timbers. We still lived aboard but spent much time ashore in a town which was just coming to life again after the German occupation. The town was still being bombarded with German V1 rockets.

These were known as flying bombs with rocket propulsion and small wings and explosives in the nose. So long as you could hear the thunder of the engine you were all right but when the engine stopped it then headed for earth. The reverberation of these explosions often loosened the timbers holding the ship upright and they had to be checked regularly. Those were scary days but we were lucky and got away with a new bow to carry on crossing and re-crossing the English Channel.

CHAPTER FIVE

My final fling as a merchant seaman was by far the most exciting and interesting as well as the longest of any of my voyages, 18 months, and to parts of the world which I had not previously visited, the Middle and Far East. This was on the M.V. Floristan, a comparatively new vessel where I had a small cabin of my own. I had already advanced to Second Radio Officer which meant I stood the 8 to 12 watch rather than the less attractive 12 to 4 so I was able to have a normal night's sleep all the time. The ship was seconded to the M.O.D. for service in preparation of the invasion of wherever the Japanese had established themselves, Burma, Malaya, Singapore, and the East Indian Islands, etc. I cannot now remember the sequence of our many travels in the Indian Ocean, the Bay of Bengal, the Malacca Straits and the China Sea and to Japan but I had the opportunity of visiting many fascinating places.

The first of these was a passage through the Mediterranean which was no longer threatened by the enemy followed by an interesting journey through the Suez Canal with sand as far as the eye could see dotted with palm trees, camels and Arabs. Next stop was at Port Sudan, probably the hottest place I have ever been in. There I was able to go on a glass-bottomed boat for a sail over the coral reefs which were so beautiful and colourful. After a short stop at Aden it was on into the Arabian Sea and the Indian Ocean

Karachi was another interesting place where we swam at the local club a little out of the town. One evening I boarded an Arab Dhow to sail over to the far side of the harbour where there was a sandy strip of beach. After a short wait for it to get a little darker we were then able to see large turtles struggling out of the water and up the beach to lay their eggs in large holes which they dug in the sand. Their eggs were about the size of a table tennis ball and about the same colour but they had a soft shell which could be squeezed.

During a stay in Bombay I was glad to be able to visit my uncle and aunt and their two children who lived there. One of the children was Peter North who we now see from time to time and he remembers my visit to them. Madras was

The legend on the back of this photo reads "Calcutta 1945". You will see I have acquired some campaign medals as well as a full(?) set of whiskers.

not much of a place but it was where I first saw native boys diving for money thrown from the ship's side.

Calcutta was the place where I saw poverty at it's greatest amongst a seething population.

Rangoon and the Schwedagong Pagoda were fascinating. It was where I discovered my boyhood friend, Laurie Crawford, was stationed with the R.A.F. and I was able to meet up with him there.

On hot nights we were able to take a mattress out on deck and sleep out there for our cabins got very hot in spite of having a fan. One night I had a terrible dream that I was being washed overboard and woke to find the monsoon had broken and the rain was pouring down so I soon scuttled inside.

About this time the two atom bombs had been dropped on Nagasaki and Hiroshima which effectively caused the Japanese to surrender. Because we were all prepared to take part in an invasion of Malaya it was decided to carry the plan through so with troops and transport aboard we set sail for two tiny places on the west coast of Malaya, Port Swettenham and Port Dickson, thence on to Singapore where I paid a visit to a Royal Navy dentist to have a tooth taken out.

The Japs were now the prisoners and there were many of them on various P.O.W. duties in and around the port area of Singapore. From there we sailed to Surabaya in the Island of Java. We were the first British ship to go there following the surrender of the Japanese and I was able to watch the ceremony of their commanding officer handing over his sword to the senior army officer who was a passenger on the Floristan and who would take over command there.

A few weeks after the dropping of the atom bomb on Hiroshima we were sent there, or rather to the naval port of Kure which is nearby, although I cannot now remember exactly why but it was an experience never to be forgotten. Hiroshima lies at the southern end of Honshu, the largest of the Japanese Islands and is approached through what is called the bay of islands. This was a beautiful area, though at this time rather grisly because the Japanese had dumped all their dead from the atom bomb on many of the islands, fortunately we were not close enough to see this. Most of the Japanese naval vessels were half sunk and somewhat battered and the port was more or less destroyed and deserted by this time.

The city of Hiroshima had virtually disappeared. A few concrete and brick buildings, like a department store and the railway station were still standing but like shells. Walking past what had been a brewery the glass bottles had all melted and it was as if a sea of glass had solidified on the ground. I do not think anyone knew about nuclear fallout in those days but I do not think I have been affected for being so close to the action, now 50 years ago. There must have been some place of entertainment still in action for I remember going to a dance and meeting a Japanese girl called Tomiko who followed the Japanese custom of walking behind the men folk.

Hong Kong was our next stop on what was to prove our homeward voyage or, rather, Kowloon which is the port across the bay from Hong Kong. What a busy bustling city it was in those days with crowds of Chinese rushing about. There were none of the lofty tower blocks which have now sprouted up but I was glad to have seen it as it was.

Back for a short stay again in Singapore before setting off for a really isolated spot in the middle of the Indian Ocean. Sailing between Sumatra and Java we passed the small island of Krakatoa which sprang out of the ocean after a mighty earthquake. Our quest was to find the tiny island of Cocos or Keeling which was an outpost of the R.A.F. used as a halfway stop for flights from the U.K. to Australia. The group of tiny islands were only a few feet above water level and did take some finding. Nautical navigation was fairly accurate in those days but there were no aids like G.P.S. navigation which today can pinpoint within a very small distance. It was some little time after we had been searching that the islands were spotted so we had made it and anchored in a palm fringed bay. One of the crew, who was fishing over the side of the ship, caught a small shark which was a lovely but vicious looking creature.

As we were leaving the anchorage the First Officer along with one of the cadets took up their usual place in the bow along with some of the crew, in this case Indians. As the anchor was being hauled up by the steam windlass one of the crew drew the attention of the First Officer (or Mate) to the cadet's cap which was floating in the water. The Mate said he did not have the time to worry about that at which the Indian crewmember said the cadet was underneath the cap. Presumably by leaning over the rail to see how the anchor was coming up he had leant too far and gone over. He must have fallen about 30 feet into the ocean but came to the surface and hung onto the anchor chain until rescued.

From the Cocos Islands we sailed to Durban in South Africa which was a pleasant spot. I bought a watch there which, 55 years later, still goes and keeps good time but as it is to wind up each day it does not get used very much now. From Durban we sailed up the East African coast to Beira and then on to the spice island of Zanzibar. It is, or was in those days, the world's main supplier of cloves and it was possible to smell the island even before you could see it, so strong was the smell of the cloves. There was certainly a Sultan's Palace but I am not too sure whether there was still a Sultan when we were there. It was another very fascinating place to visit. Then on to Mombasa and so back through the Red Sea and the Suez Canal for the final leg of my final journey as a sailor boy. We landed in Liverpool where I left the employ of the Marconi Company and returned to a rather more humdrum way of life back in Bishop Auckland.

CHAPTER SIX

We are now in about August 1946. Whilst I appreciated that the life of a sailor was alright for a single man it was no sort of life for a married one, not that I then had any thoughts about marrying although I was by this time aged 23. There was the small matter of finishing my printing apprenticeship which would have fitted me for a job in the printing trade. In order to help me do a little better than carry on at M. Braithwaite & Son I approached a large and well known printing firm in Newcastle who were willing to take me on but said I must check whether the Union would agree to this. Rather short-sightedly they did not agree and said I must go back to the old firm before trying to get a job elsewhere. The equipment and practices of the firm's printing works were somewhat antiquated. Father had no formal training in the printing trade so it was not surprising that the works were more than a little behind the times. I felt that if I could get some experience in an up-to-date firm I would have a better idea how to improve things at M. Braithwaite & Son which was badly needed. The only avenue open to me was to join the Federation of Master Printers who provided various publications and forms, particularly for costing work. With father's lack of experience his efforts at costing jobs was a sort of rule of thumb. He had no idea how much time would have been spent on any job, which machine might have been used for printing it, or how much extra work by way of folding, stapling, guillotining, or other finishing process was involved. He did know the cost of the paper used but the price to the customer was sheer guess work. When I got the staff filling in time sheets for work done and machines used I discovered we had virtually been giving work away so it became necessary to gradually bump up the prices to a more realistic level. We were never on to a winner though with the antiquated equipment still in use and some pretty good work was produced in spite of these difficulties.

I was living at home, Jack had gone off to Cambridge and Derek was studying to be a doctor at Newcastle. My other interest at this time, not surprisingly, was a girl. At the beginning of the war in 1940 the girls of a school from Gateshead had been evacuated to Bishop Auckland as being less likely to seek the attentions of the German bombers. Like so many children and young people they were placed in the homes of local residents. The local schoolchildren went to school in the mornings and the evacuees went in the afternoons. At a party I met this rather tall, pretty girl called Joan with whom there developed a mutual attraction and we saw quite a lot of each other up to the time I went off to sea. We corresponded spasmodically and when on leave we met when possible though by then she worked in the Newcastle telephone exchange so was not always free. We had our ups and down's, mostly up's, and enjoyed each other's company. After the war the situation changed and we made it our business to see each other as much as possible, she often staying at Newlands Avenue for a weekend and I occasionally staying at her house in Gateshead. Courtship was something new and strange to me and was severely affected by my puritan upbringing and inbuilt inhibitions. I had been taught to revere and respect the opposite sex, which I had always done, but now other attitudes were being required of me. With infinite patience and gradual coaxing courting took on a new dimension and our affair seemed to be flourishing, but courting at 30 miles distance has its drawbacks.

30 miles in the opposite direction was the town of Stokesley where Rev. Bertram Dewhirst was now the Methodist minister. His daughter Jean had been encouraged by my mother to correspond with we three boys and I had received a few letters from her during my travels. My parents had kept up a friendship with the Dewhirst's with whom they met from time to time so I was drawn together with Jean who I had not seen for some time. I looked upon her as a jolly friend with whom I was able to be at ease and have some good fun and when an occasion arose that I was invited to take a friend to a Rotary Ball in Bishop Auckland I asked Jean who did me the honour of being my guest. That night changed my life and was probably the best decision I have ever made. When we got home after the ball we were sitting in the kitchen at Newlands Avenue when something, I know not what, prompted me to say "I wonder what would happen if I was ever serious with you". She suggested I try it, which I did, and it was not long before we were in each other's arms, a good deal more snugly than we had been at the ball. To give some indication that all was not as well as it should be with Joan I was also seeing one of the nurses who had tended me when I was in hospital in Newcastle and, in fact, had arranged a date with her before the aforementioned incident. Many years later she somehow or other discovered we were living in north London as was she and we did meet up on one occasion. So, after some 6 years of being with Joan I was now with Jean and I felt pretty awful about telling Joan but there was nothing for it, it had to be done. I still occasionally think of her and when I do I only hope that wherever she may be, she is happy. So came about the end of an era and the beginning of a new one.

Jean and I soon became engaged. We bought a ring at a jewellers in Darlington for the princely sum of £25 and she was still wearing it on the day she died. Jean was working in a nursing home near Middlesbrough so we got together whenever we could and soon decided we should marry.

We obviously needed somewhere to live so I had done some house hunting, eventually coming up with a terraced house in Albert Hill which was being sold by auction. There was only one other buyer interested in the property which I managed to purchase for the sum of £1,275. Having saved money while at sea I was able to pay a deposit and also to buy the necessary furniture for the house. This was still special utility wartime manufacture but a good deal more solid than a lot which is on the market today. We still dine off the same table, use the same sideboard, and sleep in the same bed albeit with replacement mattress. Linen was on coupons and difficult to come by but with the help of family and friends we were able to set up a habitable home. It was a good family house although it was lit by gas and had no bathroom so we had to have electricity installed and had a fourth small bedroom turned into a bathroom.

From left to right are my father Frank, my mother Muriel, twin brother Derek as best man, myself and Jean, a bridesmaid whose name I forget and Jean's parents Marian and

Bertram. The junior bridesmaid is Barbara Heslop who lived near us and whose father was an usher.

The wedding was at Stokesley on 27th October 1948, a cold frosty morning with a bright blue sky. Derek was my best man and Jean's father took part in the proceedings which were followed by a wedding breakfast in the hall behind the church. We took the train to London that same day and spent our first married night at a hotel there. The following day we went on to Eastbourne. Imagine our surprise and disappointment when we were shown into a room with twin beds. Most nights we were able to manage with the one!. We had our food ration books with us and were able to buy a joint of meat to take home with us, otherwise we would have lost that particular ration. We also bought a second hand lounge suite in a shop in Eastbourne and a stair carpet in a shop in London on the way home.

The daily routine back in Albert Hill was breakfast, to work for the morning, (to the printing works or, rather more often now, to the shop) return for mid-day dinner, back to work, then home for high tea and, before bed, a light supper. Having spent most of my savings on setting up a home, income became a problem which Jean managed to juggle because my weekly wage was £7 from which we had to pay the mortgage on the house before anything else. Groceries and coal were the main items of expenditure. The kitchen fire had a back boiler to heat the water so that was an essential and if we moved into another room a fire was usually necessary although most of the time we lived in what was quite a large kitchen.

Having been a midwife and having watched over the travail of childbirth for so many times had not put Jean off wanting to have a child herself. Our, or more probably her, plans for a spring baby happily materialised and on April 11th 1950 our daughter Patricia Dewhirst was born in the maternity home at the top of Princes Street. In those days childbirth was followed by about two weeks lying in bed so I visited each evening to an open ward with about 6 or 8 nursing mums in it.

Jean's father sold a family ring which had been left to her and with the proceeds was able to buy a pram and a piano which Jean enjoyed playing. Jean's parents were also largely responsible for providing Jean with her major clothing requirements, coats and dresses, which was a great help to us.

The Methodist church figured quite large in our lives with Jean in the choir and I in a number of offices including Sunday school teacher and, following in father's footsteps, Quarterly Meeting secretary. Under the influence of the young minister at that time I made the mistake of believing I had been called to preach and followed the course of training to become a lay preacher. Having qualified, I, like the other 'local preachers', was required to take my share of services around the circuit churches some three, four or five times each quarter. This often meant leaving home after an early lunch on Sunday to catch the bus to some outlying church for an afternoon and an evening service before catching the bus home again. This was very unfair on Jean but there was not a lot I could do about it. Through the recommendation of Jean's father who, by this time, had become Chairman of the Middlesbrough and Darlington District of churches I was invited to become treasurer of the Overseas Missions department of the District which Involved District meetings and twice yearly journeys to the Methodist Mission House in Marylebone Road in North London. At the home church I was also involved in operating a cinema projector for an occasional 'film service' so one way and another the church kept me busy.

The church also provided us with a wonderful circle of friends, the remaining ones with whom we still keep in contact to this day. As well as occasional church social occasions we would visit each other's homes for the simple pleasures of those heady days before the advent of TV.

When Jean suggested we have another child I felt sure we could not afford to feed and clothe another baby but, as usual, in the important decisions she won the day and in June of 1952 along came John Matthew, in the same nursing home and the same two week stay. As infants Pat was outgoing whereas John was shy and clung to his mum but fortunately he grew out of that.

A nail in the coffin of the printing works was the sudden death of heart failure of the foreman. A replacement was soon found although he did not have the same dedication to the firm, or the level of experience so it became more difficult to accept certain work which we had previously done. The stationers and booksellers shop was one of the oldest properties in Bishop Auckland standing on the corner of the market place and the main shopping street. No money had been put into modernising it and, while it kept going as it was, it became increasingly clear that the business could not support two families. As a brash young man who 'knew it all' I was becoming increasingly critical of father's way of running the business and we did not get on terribly well. His health was not too good, he having smoked for most of his life, so I approached our accountant to ask what the situation for father would be if we were to sell the business and let him retire. It was felt he could retire fairly comfortably so I set about wondering what to do and applied for one or two other jobs without success. When father found out I was looking for other jobs he was very distressed and upset but I was fed up with things as they were and had got itchy feet. So M. Braithwaite & Son which was founded by my great, great grandfather and had served five generations of Braithwaites was sold.

I have to add at this point that brother Derek had gone out to Northern Rhodesia as a Doctor from where he returned every three years for a long leave. At the end of one of them which coincided with the sale of the old firm, he very generously left us the money he had not spent on his leave and this released us from a fairly hand-to-mouth existence. Derek was idolised by Pat and John in those days because he was able to play with them when on leave and he has been generous to us on more than one occasion which we have repaid with hospitality whenever we were able to give it. I should probably add at this point that on some of these long leaves which Derek had we would join him for camping holidays in France, Switzerland or Italy which was great for us all to enjoy foreign travel which we could not otherwise afford.

Not finding another job locally it became necessary to look further afield so we switched from taking the Daily Mail to the Daily Telegraph which was, and still is, well known for its appointments section. The furthest afield I tried was with a newspaper in Kenya. Eventually I answered an advertisement from W. & G. Foyle for a departmental manager which involved a trip to London and an interview with the famous Christina Foyle and her husband Ronald Batty. They were both fairly hard cases but for better or worse they offered me a job which, of course, involved a move to London. Looking for a house in London is like looking for the proverbial needle in a haystack so one has to settle on a possible area. We needed a place with good communications to Charing Cross Road and, as good Methodists in those days, believed that Muswell Hill area would fill the bill. Having left Pat and John in the care of our good friend Winsome Hutchinson we borrowed Jean's father's car and drove to London to go house hunting having previously been in touch with the Methodist minister at Muswell Hill telling him of our projected move. He kindly went round various houses with us offering good advice about each one with added comments about the local area. It seems hardly believable but in our two-day stay in London we settled on a house and paid a deposit on it. If I remember aright the house was £3000 so we were now on the ladder. The family could not move until we had sold the Bishop Auckland house so it was necessary for me to find temporary accommodation in London until we could take possession of the new house in Clifton Road which was close to a recreation ground, Alexandra Palace, Bounds Green tube station on the line to Charing Cross Road, and close to schools for the children so we were very fortunate in our choice. During this visit to London we drove into town in the evening and discovered there was something going on at the Odeon in Leicester Square. Cars were parked everywhere around the square so we parked there as well. When we got back to where the car should have been it had gone and we were panic stricken for it was not our car. Fortunately there was someone who told us we had just missed the police removing it. We rang Scotland Yard to find out where it might be and were told it was probably in a police car pound at Kentish Town where there was a tube station to which we made our way. The police there said we would probably be hearing more about the matter but did allow us to take the car away and to the hotel where we were staying a couple of nights. We had actually got to bed when Jean suggested that, because the police had damaged the driver's window to get into the car and it would not lock, it was not safe to leave it outside the hotel all night. Up we got and I went and settled our bill with the hotel and we drove north through the night with a rest stop somewhere on the way.

The daughter of a minister who had been in Bishop Auckland was living in the East London Mission in East London and she found me a room there for a few weeks while Jean was left to cope with Pat and John (aged about 8 and 6) and the sale of the old house. The move was carried out successfully and we soon settled in to a new house and a new routine. It was a terraced house set on a hill with several steps up to the front door and a small garden sloping up from the house at the back. It was a 10 or 15 minute walk to the tube station or, on a bad morning there was a bus I could catch and I soon got used to the life of a commuter, often like a sardine on a packed train.

Both sets of parents were still alive so it would have been a wrench for them to see their grandchildren taken 250 miles away. It also meant we both, or more often just Jean and the children, made occasional flying visits to the North to see them. Our parents did visit us at Clifton Road to see us settled in there but it was not long after this that Jean's mother died. Derek had very kindly left us the car he had bought to use during one of his leaves from Zambia which, of course, was a godsend for us.

At Foyle's I was instructed to take charge of Department One which covered fiction, biography, English Literature and Criticism (about which I knew very little) and Classics. With no introduction to any of the staff which numbered about 8, mainly students, I was thrust into this strange environment in the heart of London's busy book world. The most helpful body of men were the representatives of the various publishers who obviously knew a lot more about the "Foyle's" than I did and while I was not responsible for giving subscription orders for new books I had to ensure we had a sufficient and comprehensive stock of all relevant titles. The bookshop was a Mecca for book thieves who, I am sure, stole books to order for the less scrupulous smaller booksellers in the area. If we secured a conviction against a book thief we were rewarded with a £5 note which was a very welcome addition to our income. I had many "fivers" in my two and a half years with Foyle's and have been known to chase a thief several streets before catching him and hauling him back to the shop. These were the professionals, the amateurs I was more tolerant with and usually dealt with them before they left the shop with a red face and instructions not show their faces in it again. Christina

Foyle was probably devoid of any compassion because she could sack an employee with no good reason and often did, so it was a rather nerve racking existence with the threat of dismissal ever present.

"Here I am in Foyle's flanked on the left by William Foyle and on the right by Ionides (the Snake Man, with several snakes) publicising his book. I handled some of the snakes and so did some of the customers. One of these, a girl, must have mishandled one because it bit her and Ionides had to release her. Before very long there were Evening Standard newspapers on the street bearing the headline "Snake bites girl in Charing Cross Road". Fortunately this was in the days before litigation for damages was rife.

After a couple of years I decided to look around for a safer, if not necessarily a better, job and asked the book reps. for possible openings resulting in interviews with several publishers but without success. My next big mistake was to obtain a position of Assistant Manager at the bookshop of the Baptist Church, the Carey Kingsgate Press, in Southampton Row. This involved running the bookshop with 2 or 3 staff and doing some office work which included managing the ordering and despatch of the weekly "Baptist Times". The

Manager was reluctant to share any other information with me and I also found him difficult to like so it wasn't much good staying there for too long although it was two stops nearer home on the tube.

Once again I was on the lookout for another job so I moved to work for a small independent publisher called Rupert Hart-Davis who was such a nice man after several not so nice ones. I was warehouse manager with a staff of three men to pack and despatch books to customers and maintain sufficient stock of their titles to do this. Mr. Hart-Davis threw in his lot with an American publisher which was all right for a while but, alas, the whole thing fell apart and Rupert Hart-Davis had to close. Fortunately Mr. Hart-Davis did what he could to find jobs for the staff and he directed me to have an interview with Frank Herman of Methuen Publishers in Essex Street, off the Strand. This was in the stock control department so I had to learn another aspect of the publishing trade, one which I readily took to and enjoyed. The stock of books was at an independent warehouse in North London so there was no physical involvement with the books. Some time after I joined Methuen's, the stock control manager was transferred to Paper Buying and I took his place. Shortly after I joined them, Methuen's was absorbed into Associated Book Publishers which was in the process of being formed and included 5 or 6 different publishers. The stock was now very large and it was decided that A.B.P. could run its own storage and distribution warehouse which was established in Andover in Hampshire.

During this time we were heavily involved in the life of the Methodist Church in Muswell Hill. The children were soon being taken to Sunday School and Jean was soon in what was quite a good choir. I continued my preaching in the North London area and occasionally went on the 'Gospel Wagon' which involved car loads of local preachers going off to village chapels in Hertfordshire and Buckinghamshire to help them out.

I have been persuaded to include an incident which happened whilst we were in Clifton Road where opposite to us lived a pair of spinsters of uncertain age. Early on one of the mornings when Jean was at work on night duty there came a rattling on the front door which I opened to find one of the ladies from across the road asking if Jean was available. When I replied that she was not available she then asked if I could come and help her. She explained that she could not get her sister to take her morning tea and would I come and see if there was anything I could do. I duly went across the road with her and up the stairs to a bedroom. Although I had seen dead bodies I had no great experience with them but it was immediately obvious to me that the lady sitting in a chair beside the bed was quite, quite dead. Apparently her sister had got her out of bed and had sat her in the chair before trying to get her to drink a cup of tea. How on earth she could not have known her sister was dead I shall never know but that was how it was. I suggested she get herself a cup of tea and I would see what had to be done. I went back across the road to phone Jean to ask her if she could come and what should I do. She would come as soon as possible but in the meantime I was to lay the lady out on her bed and see her mouth an eyes were closed. How I brought myself to lift this cadaver from the chair and onto the bed I shall, again, never know but I did and tied her mouth shut with a scarf I found. Wasn't I glad when Jean eventually turned up and took over the grisly task.

When we came to leave Muswell Hill I was Sunday School Superintendent and I also had a District job again in the Overseas Missions Department of the Church. Jean also took a part time job at the local cottage hospital to help our finances and both Pat and John having done well at school had moved on to secondary education while we were there.

CHAPTER SEVEN

On a visit to Andover we viewed several houses which were capable of providing accommodation for my father, who was due to come home from Zambia where he had been staying with Derek for some time, and had no home to return to. We settled on 15 London Road, a gracious old house built of puddled chalk with a damp basement, a gently sloping roof and gardens at both back and front, the back one with a lawn large enough to have a cricket pitch on.

Jean and the children were not at all keen on the idea of a move to Andover as they had been so happy and settled in Muswell Hill. We drove down there one afternoon after having seen our furniture into a van in Clifton Road which would be delivered the following day. We spent the night in the lounge, one of us in each corner of the room on the floor. I remember when I got up to make a cup of tea the following morning I was thrilled to see the number and variety of birds in the back garden. We soon got settled in after which our first call was to the Methodist Church in Bridge Street where, unfortunately, we had a fairly cool and unfriendly reception. As good Methodists in those days we persevered and over time we came to be accepted and a few people became friendly in a sort of reserved way. All this changed with the arrival of a new minister to the Andover Circuit about which more later.

The new ABP building had not been completed when we moved so for the first 5 or 6 months I was a daily commuter from Andover to London Waterloo. As soon as there was accommodation for book stocks in the new Andover warehouse I had the difficult job of juggling the book stocks between two locations so that there were enough books left at the old place to service our customers and also sufficient stock at the new place to commence serving customers from there. Once that had started and all the stock was at Andover it was comparatively easy.

With a staff of 5 stock controllers I was responsible for ensuring stocks of all A.B.P. titles were adequate to meet prospective demand, to arrange for the binding up of sheet stock when necessary, and to notify editors when stock of their particular titles would be exhausted within a certain time. It was a happy working environment with my managerial colleagues being a good lot of lads. There was a canteen where I had a modest mid-day meal and our house was only a mile from the office so there was no long travelling involved.

When father arrived back from Zambia after his stay with Derek the situation became difficult for Jean. He was pretty poorly, fairly immobile, and quite demanding. He had his own room and we had incorporated an old outside toilet into his quarters so, unless we sometimes took him out in the car he seldom went out of his own quarters. We believe he was as happy that way as being involved with the family for he showed little interest in the children. He had his own television and watched mostly cricket. He never played the piano again. Because it was necessary to help him to the toilet it was not possible to leave the house for more than a couple of hours which placed great restrictions on Jean's activities and tended to colour her whole attitude to our early years in Andover.

After about 5 years he was getting more and more difficult and demanding we broached the possibility of him going into a nursing home. He had had short spells in a home whilst we went on holiday and seemed to be as happy there as with us so eventually he was settled in a nursing home in Nether Wallop, some 8 miles from Andover where he was visited regularly and where (when we were living back in Surrey) he died at the age of 92.

Pat and John both attended Andover Grammar School and got to know many friends there amongst whom was Michael Walton. He had a sister who was our family doctor who lived with her mother in Andover. Her mother, Margaret, was a widow and she attended Bridge Street Methodist Church so they became, and Margaret remains, our firmest friends of that period. Sadly, Dr. Pam Walton died of a brain haemorrhage aged 52 which was a terrific blow to Margaret who had already lost two other children and her husband in equally sad circumstances.

With the arrival of Rev. Leslie Groves the life of the church changed considerably. He was, in fact, over dedicated to his calling and made great use of our past knowledge of other churches, of Jean's very hospitable nature, and of my services whenever he could. It all got a bit too much but we bore with it while we were there I ended up in the top job of Circuit

Steward along with, for a while, another good friend we had made in the person of Brian Dancer (who was to be something of a saviour to me in later life as you shall see). He and his wife Ann, a bright and lively character, and their 3 children lived in a village outside Andover, Vernham Dene, which had an active village hall where dances were held. We went to several of them dressed variously as 'tramps and vamps' or 'Romans' etc. and had enormous fun. One of my stock control girl clerks lived in Vernham Dene and, dressed as a tramp, I approached her mother in the local pub. It took some persuasion to assure her I was who I said I was. Whilst in Andover Derek invited Pat out to Zambia for a holiday where she was joined by Dr. Pam Walton who would have liked to take a sabbatical out there but her practice partners would not let her leave which was a disappointment for her. Similarly, when John got his degree Derek invited him out to Zambia for a holiday where he had a great time. On his home leaves every three years Derek would spend a lot of time with us between visits to his other friends in the UK and Europe.

Next door to our house, on the other side to the blind home, was Andover's football ground. Saturday afternoons were quite often noisy occasions. Twice yearly the travelling fairground would descend on the town and set up its stalls, dodgem cars, swing boats and other rides over our garden wall so we had all the fun of the fair virtually on our doorstep. During one visit the puppy spaniel we had must have picked up a piece of coconut which somebody had thrown over the wall because from being a strong healthy boisterous pup he went to skin and bone. On our second visit to the vet he found an obstruction in Trampus's intestine which required an operation to remove it. He soon recovered but later, during a spell in kennels during our absence, he escaped from a gate left open and was, sadly, killed on the A3.

When the time came for Pat to leave school she opted to follow in her mother's footsteps and go into nursing. She applied to train at Great Ormond Street Hospital and was accepted on the understanding that, until she was old enough to commence her training, she should continue her education and try and have some work experience. For the latter she helped out at the blind home which was next door to where we lived until the time came for her to head for London and a nursing career.

John went on to Hendon Polytechnic to study geography and got his degree. His part time jobs included being a delivery boy on a bicycle for a local greengrocer, working at clearing an old sewage farm site, and drying grass seed for a local farmer as well as a part time postman at Christmas.

I must leave Pat to tell any tales about her doings in London during her nursing training, probably the less we know about them the better. Having 'kept company' with more than a few Andover swains she became engaged to one who we were not at all happy with. Fortunately it did not last because whilst in London she met Philip Hartwell who she eventually married.

So, perhaps the most important event during our time in Andover was the wedding of Pat and Phil in the Methodist Church followed by a reception at a local hotel. Pat's grandfather took part in the service. After a two night honeymoon in the New Forest somewhere Pat and Phil flew out to Australia 3 days after their wedding and we wondered if we would ever see them again. Phil's one promise to us was that he had enough money to send Pat home again if she was unhappy out there. Again, she must tell you of her time out there but we had regular letters and photos from them which we always shared with Phil's parents whom we had got to know very well. We would entertain each other in our homes or, sometimes, meet up at Newbury which was almost halfway between Oxford, where they lived, and Andover.

Another important development in my life happened in Andover when I was nominated by the Methodist minister and the library manger to be a magistrate. This was the second time this had been suggested to me and previously I had declined but this time I accepted. Following an interview with the town clerk I was appointed by the Lord Chancellor as a Justice of the Peace for the Borough of Andover, taken the loyal oath, and sworn in. The magistrates' court initially was held in the Guildhall in the centre of the town which was totally inadequate for this purpose. There was the actual courtroom (which doubled as concert platform, dance hall, you name it) and a small retiring room for the magistrates to discuss their findings. Solicitors, defendants, witnesses, policemen, all had to mill about on the stairs leading up to the courtroom. We usually sat with 5 magistrates which was unwieldy. With a lot of soldiery in the vicinity there was a fair amount of petty crime, some considerably worse and, during my five years in Andover, 5 murders. Towards the end of my time in Andover a new purpose built courthouse was erected, opened unofficially by Lord Denning and officially by Princess Alexandra. My highest rank was as Deputy Chairman of the Juvenile Panel. I also sat on appeals at the opulent crown court building in Winchester and it was always interesting to watch a judge at work although we were as equals on the bench and two magistrates could, and occasionally did, overrule the decision of the judge.

John, having finished his studies, decided to travel before getting a job and he too set sail, or rather, took flight for Australia. I had managed to get him a job with the Australian arm of ABP where he worked for much of the time he was in Sydney. So, for the first Christmas since Pat was born we were without our children.

I could also add at this point that, financially, we were considerably better off than we had previously been and were able to afford foreign holidays the first of which, giving Jean her first experience of both flying and Mediterranean weather, was to the Spanish Island of Ibiza. We had two self-catering cottage holidays with our friends Margaret and Pam Walton, one to Derbyshire and another to St. Just near Land's End.

It came as something of a shock to me that the firm I had worked for to the very best of my ability for 12 years, and which I had very much enjoyed working for, decided to make me redundant. It was a fairly traumatic time as you can guess. There seemed little prospect of finding appropriate employment in or around Andover so I looked back to London to see what I could find to do. I was 52 years old and obviously not the best bet for many employers. Redundancy pay helped to fill the gap in loss of salary but would not last for ever.

After some time I answered an advertisement from Pitman Publishers who were looking for a Trade Manager and had an interview for the job which I got. It turned out to be another of my less satisfactory moves for I was not able to stay with them for very long. My work there involved dealings with booksellers anxious to obtain Pitman publications and having difficulty in doing so. Distribution of their books was through Book Centre, the very organization which my previous employers had left to set up their own distribution centre in Andover. Their operation left something to be desired but Pitman's own activities weren't of the best and they were, additionally, in the process of being computerised which is seldom an easy operation. We also dealt direct with the public and had a mini book store in the basement from where small parcels of books were dispatched It just seemed to be a bit of a shambles and after my boss had interfered with my way of running my part of the operation on too many occasions I called him into my office and told him what I thought about him. My boss was a small chap with an odd manner and although I am not perhaps the easiest of people to get on with I found him rather difficult. Small men are often bossy types and he was one of these. I could hardly stay there under these circumstances so I immediately looked around again for another job, my eighth I think.

During this time Jean was spending a lot of time looking around for somewhere for us to live. All we knew was we wanted a property which had easy access to Waterloo Station which was as good as anywhere to get to Pitman's which was in a street off Kingsway, near Holborn tube station. We had managed to sell the house in Andover so ended up with having nowhere to call home. A very good friend from our Muswell Hill days with whom we had kept in touch offered us the use of her flat in Muswell Hill during the week but she would need it at the weekends. She worked in Eastbourne during the week. Our furniture had gone into store and we lived out of suitcases. At weekends we usually invited ourselves to stay with friends who were very accommodating to our needs.

It was at this time that Pat and Phil returned from Australia, via New Zealand and then across America, to take up their lives in England and it was also at this time, April 15th 1976 that Pat presented her husband with their first child and us with our first granddaughter, Sarah. Unfortunately she became very ill and spent time in hospital until it was discovered she was a coeliac, (allergic to the gluten in flour) since when she bounced back to life again. She was born in Oxford as Pat and

The house we eventually chose was in the Hinchley Wood area of the Surrey town of Esher which we moved into in 1976 and lived in for 37 happy years.

Phil were also looking for somewhere to live and they finally settled in Brockworth in Gloucestershire which is more or less equi-distant between Gloucester and Cheltenham where they still live and where we have spent many happy days in the ensuing years.

Casting around for a job I contacted Brian Dancer who, you may recall, we were very friendly with in Andover. He had become manager of Barclays Bank in Maidenhead which had amongst its customers an outfit by the name of Fairholt Printing Corporation. A somewhat grand name for the parent company of some 7 different printing or paper merchanting companies. He told me they were looking for a mature person to shadow, help, support their Company Secretary and suggested I make an appointment for an interview at their Sunbury on Thames head office which I did. I discovered that this involved dealing with a company car fleet of 40 odd vehicles, two different pension schemes and organising the firm's various insurances none of which I had any experience of. My first meeting at the Sunbury office was on 3rd May 1977 with the chief executive, Robert (Bob) Russell, a man I came to respect and admire for his handling of difficult situations and really holding the group together in spite of its Chairman. Then I met the Company Secretary, Roy Cantwell, with whom I felt I could get along. Not, as I said, having any experience of any of company secretarial affairs I was surprised to be given the offer of a job subject to a meeting with the Chairman to confirm this. I duly presented myself at the Chairman's office in Pont Street on 12th May for my meeting with Mr. James Anthony Boyden of Dewlish Hall in Dorset and after some discussion he said he approved my appointment on two counts, one that I had been recommended by Brian Dancer and two, that I was a magistrate. Incidentally on my move to London I had been able to transfer my position as a magistrate to the local court in Walton on Thames where, at the age of about 65, I was elected to be chairman of the bench which position I filled for the accepted period of three years (perhaps more of this anon).

During the period of my chairmanship there came an invitation to attend a garden party at Buckingham Palace which was quite an experience. The palace gardens are beautiful and it was fun to see what happened on these occasions. We wandered round the gardens for a while until it was time for the royal party to emerge and mingle with the crowds. Mingle is not quite correct for we were very gently shepherded into two groups both leaving an avenue for royalty to pass down the middle and meet pre-determined people and groups. The Duke of Edinburgh came down past us. We saw a goodly number of cabinet ministers making their way to a special tent where the royal party joined them for tea while we had ours in a separate marquee. We were told where we could stand to see the royal party move back to their quarters and were able to see the Queen and others pass by us very close. Jean enjoyed walking back through the palace and out into the forecourt where, for once, we were on the inside looking out at the crowds watching what was going on from behind the railings

My diary for this time shows that Jean and I had a holiday in Ireland for the last 10 days of May '77.

In November of 1977 our second grandchild, Emma Louise, was born and within a very few days Jean's father died up in Kendal where we went for his funeral.

I joined Fairholt on Monday 13th June in 1977 so started life at Sunbury which was difficult at first with new things to learn and strange people to get to know. It took me some time to get into the job but when I did I really enjoyed the work and the people. However, it turned out to be one of the better, if not the best, of all my many jobs and provided a happy and satisfactory close to my working life. As someone from 'head office' I was always treated well by the various personnel at the different companies in the group. They were as far apart as Eltham in S.E. London, Reading in Berkshire, Liphook in Hampshire, Poole in Dorset and Stevenage in Hertfordshire so there was quite a lot of travelling to do on company business.

My diary shows visits during the first two months of the job to Stevenage, Liphook, Bordon, Greenford, Eltham, Vauxhall, Reading, Stevenage, Vauxhall, Reading, Bordon, Reading, and although journeying not always quite so regularly is was an indication of the interest and variety of both the work and the people I met. Some were visits in connection with pension affairs, others concerned with insurance matters and, at a later date, others involved board meetings at the various company premises. On 6th December I did a round trip from Sunbury to Greenford/Reading/Poole/Bordon/ Liphook and back to Sunbury, a distance of 286 miles. On the following Tuesday a similar trip from Sunbury to New Eltham/Brixton/Vauxhall Street/Victoria/Stevenage/Pont Street/ and back to Sunbury, 129 miles.

In August '78 the Company Secretary's office moved to Pont Street in West London where the Chairman had his office. This involved a train to Wimbledon then a tube to Sloane Square which was about 10 minutes walk from the office. Sometimes Roy Cantwell, who invariably drove to the office, would give me a lift and Jean always knew when this occurred because I came home with my clothes smelling of pipe smoke.

In November '78 father died, aged 92, at the nursing home in Nether Wallop where he had spent his final years and was cremated at Salisbury.

January '79 saw a rail strike which made getting to work horrendous and I see I missed some of it by getting 'flu and being off work for 10 days.

In March it was back to the Sunbury office again but it was while I was at Pont Street that Tony Boyden mounted his challenge for the America's Cup with his newly constructed boat "Lionheart" which, sadly, didn't win. Yugoslavia was our holiday destination in May and by the sheerest coincidence our neighbours across the road, Betty and Cecil Fitzwilliam were on the same planes but not at the same resorts.

During this time Jean had been working part time at the Home of Compassion, a local nursing home, in an attempt to get to know people in our new locality and we both became fairly involved with the activities of the Home. I was treasurer of the Friends of the Home for a number of years and so involved with regular committee meetings, fund raising activities, summer fairs, jumble sales and other events.

Our membership of the National Trust stems from April 80 when we visited Stourhead with Margaret and Pam Walton and were persuaded to become members. We have never regretted this and remain members to this day, able to freely visit N.T. properties in whatever part of the country we find ourselves. As a National Trust volunteer steward myself at the time this is being written I am interested to see our 'Recruiter' at Clandon Park at work seeking new members.

Italy was our chosen holiday destination in '80 with 7 days in Rome and 7 days in Sorrento. Derek was able to come along with us and renew his memories of the country he had spent some time in during the war. We had a boat trip to the lovely Isle of Capri, a visit to the Roman excavations at Herculaneum, and a visit to Naples.

On April 24th 1981 our third, and probably the last, grandchild was born to Pat and Phil. A boy this time, Andrew John. The year was special in a way because at the end of April there was a very heavy fall of snow in the west country and while Phil, with the help of Jean, had to clear their drive to go and bring Pat home from the hospital, I couldn't even get to Brockworth as the M4 road was closed by snow.

I had taken on an allotment about ¾ of a mile from home and about this time the local council were encouraging self-management of their allotment sites, a move which I became involved in at an inaugural meeting at a local school. Along with two or three other fellow plot holders we agreed to hold a meeting of as many plot holders as were interested to discover their views on such a move. Most of them could not have cared less, they only wanted to get on with running their plots, so we agreed to go self-managed. This meant quite a lot of legal work concerned with drawing up a suitable lease which meant meetings at the council offices. We eventually agreed terms and finished up with a 25 year lease on our allotment site with myself as chairman, with a secretary and a treasurer as the three trustees. We needed to set plot rental rates and a system to collect these. We were statutorily required to hold an AGM and had to pay the council a proportion of the rental gathered. Before I eventually gave up my plot which was becoming too much hard work I had three changes of secretary and three changes of treasurer. I keep my links with the Sugden Allotment Association through several of my old colleagues there but was happy to see the system well on its way before I, too, departed from the scene.

As well as working at the local nursing home to get to know people Jean also answered an appeal in the local newspaper for people to join the committee of the Esher Branch of the Guide Dogs for the Blind Association and was welcomed with open arms. After some little while it transpired the secretary would be moving out of the district so a replacement was needed. I offered to help and I, too, was welcomed with open arms. So began a period of some 17 years during which the Branch sent about £250,000 to headquarters as the result of street collections, collecting boxes, visits to fairs and fetes, talks to local groups, etc.

We were often going to and fro to Brockworth to see our family and to watch the grandchildren grow up.

My diaries towards the end of the '80's and the beginning of the '90's are pretty full of meetings in relation to the affairs of the magistrates court system for the county of Surrey for I had been elected as a member of the Magistrates Courts Committee, remaining a member until my retirement from active magisterial duties on reaching age 70. I found this work very interesting although it was difficult at times to take decisions which were not always in the best interests of my own court at Walton-on-Thames. This, which I found difficult to impress on my colleagues at Walton, was because members of the Committee were not elected to represent the interests of their own court but of the interests of the whole system. I was on a sub-committee concerned with court accommodation which meant visiting all the court buildings in the county on a regular basis and deciding on alterations or improvements within strictly limited budgets. I was fortunate that my work and my employers allowed me time to do this as well as to attend court sittings about once each week or ten days.

For a few years I was also on the Police Committee for the County which was also most interesting and gave me a better insight into the problems of the police service. It also gave us invitations to police dog trials at the police HQ at Mount Browne outside Guildford which was an interesting day out. Policemen with heavily padded arm shields, firing revolvers into the air and being chased and caught by hefty German shepherd dogs.

So, work wise, I was now back at the little Sunbury office of F.P.C. with still a considerable amount of travelling to do and which I was quite happy to do. I enjoyed haggling with car salesmen about the purchase of new company cars. My predecessor had dealt solely with one dealer for all makes of car but as company directors and sales representatives had a choice of car within a certain budget it was an oddly assorted fleet of cars for which I was responsible. We had to arrange the renewal of the annual car licence for each vehicle and to advise when an MOT was due and see it was carried out. Sales Representatives cars were very prone to accidents and we dealt with all these from Sunbury. I was always suspicious of those accident report forms which put the blame for damage to a car on somebody else knocking into it in a car park. One of the most serious, and costly, accidents was when the chairman's Rolls Royce being driven by his chauffer on returning to Dewlish late at night breasted the brow of a hill and ran into a herd of cows which had escaped onto the road. The cows were hurt but the Rolls was a write off and put up our motor insurance premiums quite a lot in the following year.

On the retirement of Roy Cantwell as Company Secretary I was invited to replace him which showed more confidence in me by my employer than I had in myself. However I did agree and the first move was for the chairman to invite Roy and myself for a meeting at his country house, Dewlish Hall, in the village of Dewlish in Dorset. Here I learnt of some of the inconsistencies, which prevailed in the group and, to my surprise, some of the salaries, which directors enjoyed. We were entertained to lunch before I drove us home in my new role as Company Secretary of the main Group Board and about eight subsidiary companies.

My first main board meeting was held at the offices of our legal advisers at Lincoln's Inn where I was invited to sit alongside the chairman to take copious notes of what was said and by whom. Once back at Sunbury these were written out in longhand for my secretary to type up and submit to the chairman for approval. Although there was no lunch or dinner after this particular meeting there was very often a lunch at a restaurant after other board meetings so I enjoyed many free meals during this time. Having started out life as a printer it was strange to be finishing involved with printing but of a very different kind. The main output of W.H.Peel was Tachograph Discs for commercial vehicles and pads of art paper and other artist's materials. Another company, A.J.Plunkett, was only concerned with putting lines on paper (i.e. ruling) producing many different kinds of ruled pads, ledgers, etc. Display craft was a screen-printing company producing posters and point of display material; their main customer for a timc was B & Q for whom they did all sorts of notices, price tags, etc. Fairholt Business Forms produced multi-part continuous stationery. Precision Printing Company made printing machines but was not viable and ceased to exist during my time. Lamport Gilbert of Reading were general printers and could produce almost anything in the printed line. Gothic Press in Eltham,

S.E. London, mainly printed and produced sleeves for gramophone records. Photographic Services Ltd was a wholesaler of just that material. Berrick Brothers of Stevenage was a wholesaler of a multitude of material predominantly in the art world and was agent for many well known lines of pencils, pens and the like. The odd man out was Seagull Limited, which made outboard motors at their factory in Poole, Dorset. Unfortunately their product, good as it was, was not good enough to match the range of outboard motors being imported from Japan and they, too, went into decline. At one time there was also a company producing gramophone discs. This was situated underneath our office at Sunbury where they had a sound proof room for recording purposes. Perhaps their best-known customer was Angela Rippon who recorded Peter and the Wolf for the company.

Towards the end of my time the office became relocated at Greenford, Middlesex, which meant a rather longer journey to work but they were nice offices with the chairman situated there as well. We had not been there for too long when a change came about.

As in the case of many outfits it was difficult to generate enough cash to develop to meet the competition and it became necessary to go public. The chairman was, of course, rather reluctant to lose his position but was persuaded and the chosen route was to sell the company to a compatible buyer. Unfortunately a company which had a number of irons in the fire but which was predominantly involved in the clothing market bought Fairholt and it turned out to be the wrong one for that same company fairly soon afterwards was closed down. When the deal was completed the head office staff moved to offices in Wokingham and it was there that I finished my days with F.P.C. I had been able to reduce my working week gradually from 5 to 4 days and then from 4 to 3 days so retirement came in stages but I missed the comradeship of some very nice people with whom I had worked for a number of years.

Retirement is, of course, a major change in ones way of life. Staying later in bed in the mornings rather than getting up early and driving to work. Finding out what one's wife did all the time one was at work and being encouraged to participate in those activities but I was not a very willing learner and cleaning windows is about the only thing I regularly, or not so regularly Jean would say, get involved with. I am not much into culinary affairs although I did decide to make bread, with varying success (until we invested in an automatic bread maker), and almost always prepare the vegetables for the evening meal.

In June of 1995 family wedding bells rang again when John and Anne, who had been together for a number of years, decided it was time to get married. The service was at the parish church of Merton Park (the church where Admiral Lord Nelson had worshipped at one time and where his named pew still remains).

Four years later, in 1999, Sarah, our eldest granddaughter married (her friend since school days) Paul and thus became Mrs Grigg. Both these events were, of course, very happy family occasions

We have had a number of interesting and enjoyable foreign holidays including:

May 1979 took us to Yugoslavia, Dubrovnik and then Lake Bled.

May 1982 we sampled Tunis

May 1990 we took the car to Hamburg and drove around Denmark.

September 1991 the Scilly Isles were our destination.

September 1992 started with a family reunion in Edmonton from where we went on with Jack and Dorothy to Glacier Park, Yellowstone Park and all points east back to Ann Arbor

September 1993, along with Derek, we had a nostalgic holiday in North East England

June 1994 saw us walking in the Black Forest area of Germany.
September 1995 had an extended stay in the USA culminating with a family reunion in Ann Arbor.
November 1998 on the occasion of our Golden Wedding the family arranged for us to have a weekend in Venice.
September 1999 to Bruges by Euro star Train
September 2000 to Tuscany in Italy

As well as these holidays abroad we usually had one or two short Bed and breakfast breaks in all corners of the U.K.

I still had the allotment until my 77th year when I gave it up and was still involved with Guide Dogs for the blind until about the same time. Now, at 79, I tend to take life fairly easily and am more than happy with the morning paper, the crossword, my computer, and my dear wife of 53 years who is ever ready to try and get me off my chair and doing something useful about the house or garden

Taken in the Forest of Dean in 2001

CHAPTER EIGHT

I have been persuaded to continue the story of my life, so at least somebody has shown some interest in the foregoing which has made it all worthwhile. So we take it up from, let's say, Christmas 1999. This is always a time for getting together with family and friends and for this Christmas we spent a happy time with our family in Brockworth where the hospitality is always so lavish. For New Year's Eve we were home again and entertained our very good neighbours, Betty and Cecil, along with two other friends from further along the Drive. Jean provides a splendid meal and I try to organize some quizzes which meet with a mixed reception.

As things get older they tend to wear out and exactly the same principal applies to the human body so our diaries are littered with appointments with doctors, chiropodists, opticians, blood tests and the like which I won't refer to in detail. The number of attendances at funerals also increases as we continue to outlive our contemporaries. I continued my regular visits to the National Trust House at Clandon Park to do my stint, every ten days or so, as a room steward until a time which will emerge in due course and although I cannot say I enjoyed this little job, as many stewards claimed to do, I did find it interesting and certainly worthwhile. I have also continued with my marquetry and attending our little class on Monday afternoons at the local Day Centre but am running out of ideas for things to do or make. My recent major work has been to apply marquetry to our 3 tier nest of tables. For the few years that there was a Woodworker Exhibition at

Sandown Park the Club helped with a mini marquetry exhibition at that event.

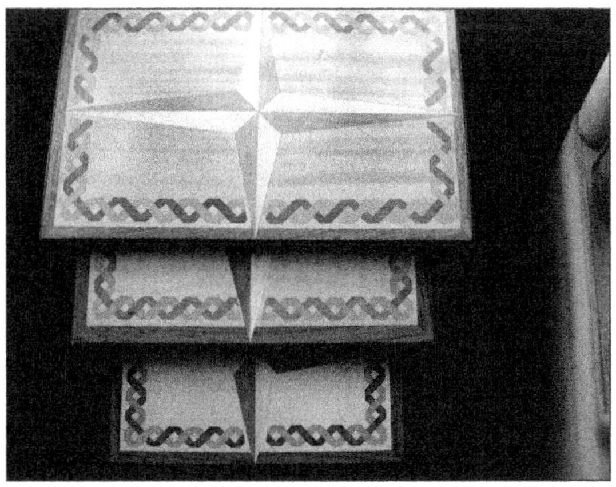

Some friends of ours have a flat in Torquay which they have kindly offered us the use of and in June of 2000 we spent a few days there during which we were able to meet up with an old friend from Muswell Hill days, Monica Lansley.

At the end of September we had a good holiday in Tuscany with visits to several well known towns of that area – Florence of course – and a generous helping of Chianti Classico to wash down our meals. In mid November a National Trust coach outing took us to the Palace of Westminster where we were fortunate enough to have a very good guide who took us up stone stairs to the Queen's robing room and through to the Lords, the voting lobbies, the Commons and finishing in Westminster Hall. Just a few days later we were off again to Brockworth for a few days during which Pat took us to Bristol where we saw the S.S. Great Britain (most interesting) and Bristol Zoo where the penguins are so much fun.

Christmas was once again at Brockworth and on New Year's Eve we paid a return visit to our friends across the road which takes us into 2001.

On January 2nd, we are now into 2001, I went into the day surgery unit at Kingston hospital for a gastroscopy to see why I was suffering from indigestion but the result was inconclusive so to deal with the problem I was prescribed a daily pill of Lansoprazole which I suppose I will continue to take for evermore. A more pleasant outing later in January was to Somerset House where there is a marvellous collection of silver, micro mosaics, and snuff boxes. There was also a mini exhibition of items from The Hermitage Museum at St. Petersburg which were fabulous.

In June, I became involved, courtesy of Pat Saunders (a friend of Jean's), with the charity The Wishbone Trust who were organizing a charity walk. It was all a bit chaotic because having offered to be treasurer for the event the committee employed a part time girl to deal with correspondence etc. who had started before I could say how I wanted to run the thing my way. The day of the walk was a bit of a shambles as walkers were having to queue up to hand in their sponsor money and a not very accurate list of these was kept. I had a lot of juggling to do to get any kind of a financial statement prepared but we did make a lot of money and any problems were happily overlooked.

Our jaunt in September was to Scotland stopping at a favourite B&B at Low Jock Scar (near Shap In Cumbria) on the way. It was my first visit to Glasgow since W.W. 2 days but of course I didn't remember any of it. We visited the Burrell Collection and also the John Rennie Mackintosh House. From Glasgow we went on to Aboyne to an old friend of Jean's who showed us something of Deeside. We were able to walk over the Balmoral Estate and to see the castle. On 10th September we stayed at a farmhouse B&B in Cupar, Fifeshire, a visit I will always remember. When we returned there late afternoon on 11th September the lady of the house rushed us into her room where the TV was showing the aeroplanes flying into the World Trade Centre in New York. I never remember where I was when John F. Kennedy was shot but I think I will always remember where I was on the infamous 9/11 as the Americans describe it. Later that month we had a short coach trip to Paris and, of course, the thing I remember about that was the driver of the coach took us into night-time Paris where we saw the Moulin Rouge with its windmill turning round. This was following an evening boat trip on the river from where we had a good view of the illuminated Eiffel Tower.

Brother Derek was still living in his own house at this time and able to drive so we had him regularly for an evening meal after which we would normally have a game of Canasta.

So 2001 drew to a close with the usual Christmas and New Year gatherings and celebrations including this year a visit to Oatlands C. of E. church with our good friends Betty and Bernard Day for their annual carol concert.

Early in January 2002 we paid a long overdue visit to the British Museum to see as much as we could.

Our Doctor's surgery boasts a Friends organization which makes money to provide the practice with extras which the NHS does not provide and over the years they have raised, and spent, over £25,000 by having "Race Nights", Quizzes etc. They have an A.G.M. each year at which, following the statutory business of the organization and an assessment of the current position of the practice vis-à-vis their thoughts on the NHS by one or more of the doctors, they have a guest speaker who has always been either interesting or amusing or sometimes both. Twice there has been a local cancer surgeon who first gave a talk, with specimens, on old medical instruments, and later a talk on more up to date medical practices including a bottle of live leeches. Another surgeon from Kingston hospital brought his guitar and gave us many of his own trite and humorous songs. We have also had the local M.P.

The lady who was treasurer of our Guide Dog Branch during most of my time with it had died the previous year but, because she was a Jewess, the family do not install a memorial stone on the grave until a year has passed. So it was interesting to go to a special Jewish section of the cemetery at Weybridge to attend the dedication of her grave stone.

Mid March saw us driving down to Cornwall for a few days B & B near St. Austell, primarily to visit the Eden Project and The Lost Garden of Heligan both of which were most interesting. We also paid a visit to a very old friend, Jane Scott (from Bishop Auckland days) and her husband who took us to lunch at one of their favourite restaurants on the Lizard peninsular.

We have four family birthdays occurring in April and this year we were at Brockworth just after Pat's and a bit before Andrew's so were able to celebrate both. Shortly afterwards we had another interesting morning on London's South Bank (the Queens Walk) beside the Thames, passing the Festival Hall, the National Theatre, Tate Modern, the Globe Theatre, the Cutty Sark and the London Clink (notorious old Jail), finishing up at Southwark Cathedral for a snack lunch at their refectory.

Our old friend Margaret Walton was still alive at this time and we occasionally had a day trip to Goodworth Clatford during which we mainly went to a local pub for lunch and sometimes took Margaret to Romsey or somewhere else for her to do a bit of shopping.

Our very good airport taxi service came into use in May when Pat and Phil went off from Heathrow to the USA for a holiday with their friends and again on their return in early June. We are also a handy car park for those going off from either Heathrow or Gatwick.

In June another few days B & B'ing, this time in Kent, near Canterbury which is always worth a visit. I achieved my life-long ambition to visit Margate and Ramsgate but what was more interesting were our visits to Dover Castle and Walmer Castle.

Another day out to London in mid May took us to the Wallace Collection and the Hayward Gallery. I am always very impressed by the wonderful marquetry of days gone by when woodworking implements and tools were so much more primitive.

The Surrey Branch of the National Trust runs a series of outings to all sorts of interesting places, often those not open to the general public, so on 12thSeptember we coached from Clandon Park to Lambeth Palace where we were dropped off at the door and given a guided tour round much of the palace, particularly the older part which includes a wonderful library. At one time the Palace was right alongside the Thames but now there is an embankment which serves to hide the sewers running beneath it.

Our main holiday of the year was with our favourite tour operators, Page & Moy, to Portugal where our first stay was in Oporto, obviously the home of Port Wine and we did visit their Bodegas for some tasting. The second part of the holiday was further up the Douro river where our hotel was right on the river bank, with a vineyard straight across from us, and every room had a river view so we were able to watch the cruise boats passing to and fro. The food was lovely and what was a nice touch were the baskets of fruit standing in the hotel corridors from which one could help oneself. From there we had an exciting train ride along a line which hugged the river bank, sometimes crossing the river. After a "pub" lunch we went on to an archaeological site. All very interesting.

Our last day out for this year was to the Queen's Gallery at the back of Buckingham Palace where a lot of Her Majesty's treasures were on show. It was a bit crowded but well worth the visit to see such magnificent works of art.

As a thank-you for having looked after their house while they were on holiday John and Anne took us for a short weekend in Dorset at the beginning of November. We stopped first at Sherbourne to look at the Abbey which we had never visited and were then driven to a little village called Evershot where we were installed in a cosy little hotel with good food. A very pleasant and welcome thank-you indeed.

And so 2002 drew to a close with the usual gatherings and Christmas festivities when it is always so good to get together with family and friends.

2003 started badly when John's father-in-law died. He and his wife lived near Lincoln so in mid January we took ourselves up there for his funeral to support the family. The 'wake' was in a local pub where I found myself sitting beside the lady vicar who had conducted the funeral. She was a young but very large lady who reminded me of Dawn French and whose appetite put mine to shame!!!

Emma was by this time in Australia so it was back to Heathrow with Pat & Phil for them to visit their daughter in Sydney. At the time when Emma was in Israel and we had visited her there Jean reminded her of this and said "don't expect us to come and visit you in Australia", but of course we did and had the holiday of a lifetime. Because we wished to visit Peter North in Tokyo we flew with Japanese Airlines which was quite OK but with any airline the journey would have been and have seemed just as long, this being the only drawback to such a visit. We had 6 hours to wait in Tokyo before the onward flight to Sydney where we landed in the early morning to find a smiling Emma with her friend's car to drive us into the city centre. While Pat and Phil were there Phil had enquired about hotels for us and settled on the Corus where one of the doormen had told Phil he would look after us – and he did, being very friendly and helpful in booking trips for us and leaving chocolate bars in our hotel room. We had the most wonderful time in and around Sydney which I am sure matches New York in so many ways. It had been 60 years since I had last been there and while the harbour and the bridge were much the same the city had blossomed like so many other capitals, although I did recognize the old Town Hall where I had been to a dance with a fellow ship's officer and a couple of Australian W.A.A.A.F.s so long ago. Our two weeks there soon passed so it was then back to Tokyo. During the flight a Japanese stewardess invited us to look out of her window as we were flying over the Barrier Reef and it was wonderful to look down on it from such a great height.

Peter, along with his Japanese friend Mikio with whom he lived, duly met us and we were taken straight out to their country cottage which has no mains supply of any kind. They have a generator which allows them to have TV and lighting while it is on but after the evening meal it is switched off and the only lighting is from oil lamps and torches strapped round the head, much like the coal miners wore the generator also pumps water up from a well. Both Peter and his Japanese colleague love their little garden there which we were shown round with pride. After the week-end it was a drive of two or three hours back to their house in Tokyo which had been only recently re-built and which was very nice. As is the custom we always removed our shoes when entering the house and donned a pair of the slippers lined up inside the door. We would never have found our own way around this vast bustling city so it was just as well we had Peter to show us the sights and the mysteries of their ever so efficient underground system. We were fortunate it was Cherry Blossom time and the trees around the royal palace had to be seen to be believed. However there were hordes of the usual pushy Japanese tourists around the site with their cameras and video recorders etc. All in all Peter helped us to make our visit a memorable one. After three weeks away it is always good to get home but we really had a wonderful holiday.

On May 15th we drove over to visit Margaret Walton in Winchester hospital which was just as well for on the 22nd she sadly passed away. A fortnight later I was pleased to be invited to read a lesson at her funeral at the local crematorium from where we went on to a memorial service at Goodworth Clatford church where, rather nicely we thought, some of her excellent pottery items were on show.

Brother Derek made an annual visit to friends (who had been in Zambia with him) in Austria and in June one of the sons of the family came over here to stay with Derek. We invited Derek and Shaun for a meal during which we discovered Derek had made no plans for entertaining Shaun so we stepped into the breech making suggestions and taking Shaun to various places including the Milestones museum in Basingstoke. Shaun spoke good English and was, I think, quite as pleased to be with us as with Derek.

The man who took over from me as Chairman of the Sugden Allotment Association, Gerald by name and a proper gardener by profession, invited us to his 60th birthday party held in the Garden Room at Hampton Court where he had served his apprenticeship 40 years earlier. He had guests from various aspects of his life, most of whom didn't know each other so after the meal Gerald spoke and, table by table, told us all what his association had been with the people on it. Such an interesting and enjoyable occasion. To this day he brings us flowers and vegetables for no reason at all except that he likes doing it – he has a heart of gold and, for a bachelor, is very outgoing.

Sadly, twin brother Derek was developing Parkinson's disease and was no longer able to maintain his house so moved into a small flat in Merrow, Guildford and I was able to help him move his possessions to his new abode. We were still having him up to our house regularly for an evening meal and a game of Canasta which was about the only outing he had apart from his regular visits to Guildford Cathedral where he operated the brass rubbing centre.

On 18th September, the very day of me helping Derek to move, Jack and Dorothy arrived at Gatwick on what was to turn out to be their very last visit to the country of their birth. As I was otherwise engaged it was fortunate that Anne offered to go with Jean to meet them at the airport. I do not have notes of all that we did with and for them but they did spend a few days at Brockworth and we took them for a tour of Buckingham Palace which was wonderful. Even then Jack was beginning to lose his memory but was very willing to go wherever we wanted to. He read and looked at the same two books over and over again but laughed loud and long with me as I put a Peter Sellars video on while

Jean and Dorothy were out somewhere. It was sad to see him like that.

To have a break after their visit we took ourselves off to the lands of our births with a B & B visit to Yorkshire and County Durham. To an old stone house in Masham (pronounced, I am always reminded, Massam) and another old stone house in the middle of Hamsterly Forest where we had lovely meals and bathed in a tiered bathroom bigger than any of our own but where the hot water took for ever to arrive through the tap.

Emma got back from Australia a few days later and we were at Brockworth for a welcome home party a few days after that.

Towards the end of the year we had another National Trust day outing, this time to see Whitehall Palace, the site of Charles I's beheading on a scaffold erected specially for that purpose. The interior of the Palace is quite beautiful and well worth a visit.

For Jean's birthday I booked a surprise B&B couple of days not far from Winchester for another pleasant break.

Because I have two leaky heart valves I have annual visits, firstly to have an E.C.G. and, secondly, to see the heart specialist at Kingston Hospital outpatients and this has been going on for a few years.

Although it was our promise to ourselves, on my retirement, that we would have a special day out every month this promise has not been fulfilled even though we obviously have the time and the resources to do so. For some reason it just didn't seem to work out and the more time passes the less we seem to try to keep our promise. Lots of little things crop up to come in the way. I get to London four or five times a year but only because I go to Moorfields Eye Hospital to have injections in my eyelids to try and prevent excessive blinking so I do not see much of the big city.

In May 2004 we went with Page & Moy for a two centre fortnight in Andalusia, Spain, which we greatly enjoyed.

It involved quite a lot of traveling by coach to various destinations, often starting early which meant breakfast at 7 a.m. but it was well worth the effort. Our first hotel was in Cordoba with its wonderful Mosque. A day trip to Granada had to include the Alhambra Palace where I took lots of photos of marvellous architecture. Then to Seville with its bullring and its pretty blue flowered Jacaranda trees. Our second hotel was on the Atlantic coast at Conil de la Fontera right on the cliff top above lovely sands. The food in this hotel was something to drool over – self service but with so much choice it was difficult to decide what to have. A day trip to Jerez gave us Sherry tasting and watching the famous horses practicing their walking and prancing. Another day took us to Ronda, a town on a hilltop divided by a steep (600 feet) and narrow gorge over which was an 18th century bridge.

Ronda also had its bullring but what was more interesting was to see the Procession of the Virgin, a Catholic religious parade across the little bridge where everyone was in their best finery and the large Virgin was carried by about 50 men in dark suits and white gloves who had to stop often to get their breath and strength back. Our last trip of the holiday was to Gibraltar and Cadiz, both very interesting. (My photographs of the above holidays are on prints in photograph albums.)

It was this year I had my second cataract operation but as my second eye was never as good as the first one it was a bit of a disappointment that the operation did not seem to have gone so well.

In May brother Derek had a fall in the middle of the night resulting in rather nasty injuries which got us out of bed after an emergency phone call at 6 a.m. to get him into Guildford hospital where we visited him for a few weeks before he was transferred to Cranleigh for rehabilitation. Two of his Austrian friends visited him in August and we had them for lunch then met them again in the evening at Derek's local pub. As we came away Susi (the doctor mother) said we must go and stay with them in Austria which, as you will see later, we did. At this time Derek was still able to drive and we were still having him weekly for an evening meal and the usual Canasta

Our autumn break was to Wales. On a previous holiday we had met up with a very friendly couple with whom we had kept in touch over the years so on our way we had a day with them in Shrewsbury which was a happy reunion. We then spent three days near Welshpool, visiting local attractions, followed by two nights near Abergavenny. The weather was not too kind so we spent some time in local caves.

2004 drew to a close with our ever happy few days with the family at Brockworth. I perhaps ought to say here that we do also see John and Anne from time to time with meals at each other's houses which are also happy times but they are both busy people with lots of their own friends who seem to keep them on the go without any help from us.

At the beginning of March 2005 we had a reunion with most of my old work mates at a pub near Beaconsfield where one of them lives and it was good to talk about old times and keep in touch with people we are happy to think of as friends.

Another old friend from our Muswell Hill days, Jean Wright, or Stacey as she now is but sadly widowed, came to stay for a few days and I see we took her to the National Trust property at Petworth which we always think of as a rather gloomy old house.

In April we had a short visit from Canadian second cousin Debi and her friend, their first visit to Europe where eventually they had seen five countries in seven days. That's how they do it!!! Their two priorities were to visit Stonehenge and the Tower of London. They arrived at Heathrow mid morning and were not too tired to make the journey so, with a picnic lunch already packed, we set straight off for Stonehenge. It was lunch time when we arrived there but they hadn't time for lunch before going off to visit the stones with their audio guide.

We took them home via Salisbury to show them that wonderful cathedral which they described, as they described so many things, as “awesome”. They did get to the Tower next day and had a good guide to tell them all about the place.

As soon as we had seen them off on the rest of their European tour we were off for our promised stay in Austria and were met at Vienna airport by Susi. Susi (a widow and a doctor by profession and still working) and her children Patrick (Paddy), Shaun (previously mentioned) and Barbara, who we had met the previous year, live in Neinkurchen, about 60 kilometres outside Vienna but with a very good rail link into the city in super double-decker trains. Susi took us in to Vienna on the first day to show us our way around and thereafter we spent a few days in the city on our own seeing some wonderful buildings and other sights. Their palaces are very ornate with lots of gilding and large chandeliers

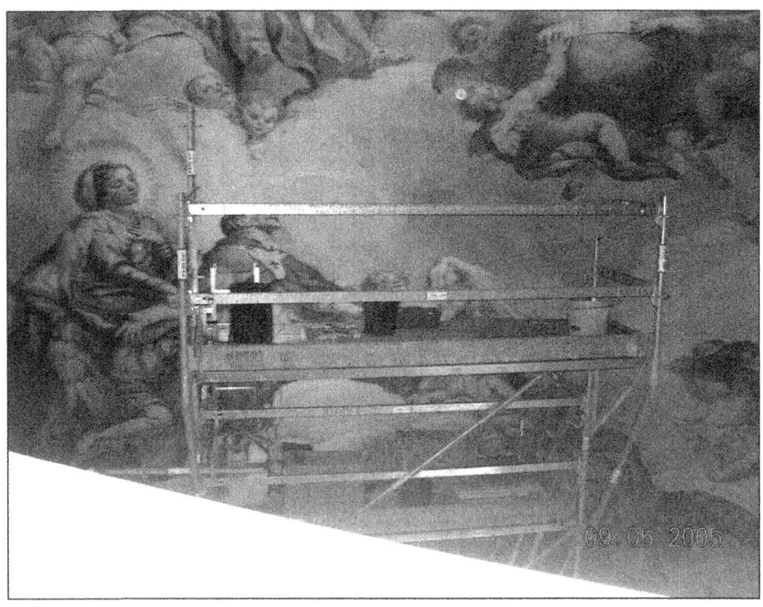

On our visit to one of the old churches where restoration was under way a lift had been installed to take workers (and visitors) right up into the large dome so we were able to see

at close hand the wonderful paintings on the dome and view the city from the lantern on top of the dome.

In June Ted, the eldest son of my niece Ann, came over from America (with his art group who were based in north-west London) spent a weekend with us during which we took him for a visit to and tour of Windsor Castle on one day, left him to make his own way round Hampton Court Palace another day and on his last day to Claremont Landscape gardens and then on for him to see Derek. He had appreciated Windsor more than Hampton Court because there were more pictures in Windsor Castle.

Thursday July 7th brought the infamous bombing of London's underground and a bus in Tavistock Square, the horrific details of which emerged in succeeding news bulletins on the television.

Monday 29th August is almost engraved on my heart for it was on this day that Jean returned from collecting the newspaper from the newsagent just a few minute's walk from our house having not been able to walk in a straight line and looking rather strange when I opened the door to her as usual. It was difficult for her to mount our door step but I got her into the house and sat down and she very soon recovered and said she was alright. I was due to make my regular visit to Clandon and hesitated about going but Jean said I should go which I did. Returning home at about 5 p.m. all seemed well and remained so until about 9 p.m. when I looked across the room to where she was putting photos into an album to see she had stopped and was looking strange again. I went across to her to find her right arm and right leg had both gone numb. This, on top of the morning's episode, prompted me to suggest we took her to A and E at Kingston to which she agreed. After spending the night in hospital she was discharged the next morning with medication to combat the two mini strokes she had had the previous day. This happening made me decide I should no longer spend days away from home so I notified the manager at Clandon that I would no longer be able to be a steward there. That concluded my twelve years service with the National Trust. A C.T. scan on Jean in September confirmed no lasting damage had been done by her mini strokes and she remains fit and well so far.

We had already booked a few days B&B holiday to visit Alnwick Castle Gardens which had to be cancelled as had a holiday in Prague.

On the last day in October I had been asked to do some shopping after my marquetry class so went to Waitrose where, as well as the things Jean had asked for, I found Croft Sherry was on cheap offer so bought a bottle of that as well. Going up the stairs back to the car I tripped on the step before the middle landing, fell, and dropped the plastic bag with the shopping in, The sherry bottle broke and I managed to cut my hand rather badly on a piece of broken glass. A lady helped me pick myself up and pointed to my hand which was bleeding profusely and made me go back down to the shop where the staff did what they could to staunch the flow of blood while calling for an ambulance as they did not have a first aider on the premises. The shop had rung Jean to tell them what had happened. First to arrive was a paramedic who cleaned the wound and bound it up tightly, then came Jean. The paramedic said he was obliged to take me to hospital so I went in his car while Jean went in ours and we met up in A and E where eventually a doctor put six stitches in my wound which still shows.

Early in November Pat and Phil took a fortnight's holiday in Egypt so, of course, we had their dogs to stay involving daily walks which we always enjoy (unless the weather is very bad). To compensate for this we were happily able to spend Christmas with them at Brockworth.

2006 was a momentous year for me as will emerge. Mid January was the annual making of some 50 pounds of marmalade to see us through the year with our breakfast confection.

February saw us re-united with old friends from our Andover days, Brian and Ann Dancer, who were off on holiday to South Africa so we invited them to leave their car with us for 3 weeks while we delivered and collected them from Heathrow. It was good to catch up with old times and it is true there are no friends like the old ones.

Jean and I had a trip to Welford Park to see their magnificent display of snowdrops followed shortly afterwards by a few days with Pat and Phil at Brockworth.

The annual show by the Hinchley Manor Operatic Society this year was "Oliver" which was well up to their usual high standard with a really cheeky Oliver and splendid Fagin.

On Friday 3rd February having experienced problems with my bowels I took myself off to the doctor who immediately sent me by "fast track" to Kingston Hospital. Ten days later I was seeing a consultant at Queen Mary's hospital at Roehampton. Such a nice man who arranged for me to have a colonoscopy investigation to see what the trouble was. This was carried out at the day surgery unit at Kingston hospital and when Jean came to collect me she tackled the doctor who had done it to discover that he thought it was very probably cancer of the bowel. Another trip to Roehampton hospital later that week where it was arranged for me to have a scan which took place on 4th April. Between all these visits life went on as usual, having a fellow marquetarian and her husband for lunch, taking Anne to Heathrow on a Sunday early morning and our old neighbours, Geoff and Jean, to Heathrow the following Saturday. Our car virtually knows its own way to the airport by now. We had planned and booked a few days holiday in Norwich at this time but that had to be cancelled.

On 10th April another visit to Roehampton to see the consultant, who had had the results of both the colonoscopy and the scan, who booked me into Kingston hospital on 24th April for him operate on the following day. We felt it was pretty good for the much maligned NHS from first seeing my GP on 3rd February to an operation 7 weeks later. The operation was a colonectomy which involved the removal of about 8 inches of cancerous bowel and then joining up the two loose ends. It is really wonderful what modern surgery can achieve and I count myself fortunate to come out at the other end of this experience as well as I was before it. However it is true to say that I hated my stay in hospital in a dark gloomy ward with hardly any daylight, very poor food but good nursing, and a revolting character in the bed opposite to me who kept waving his amputated leg in the air and kept calling for a nurse rather than using the call bell.

That though was far from the end of the story. I was glad to get home again on the 3rd of May and had the clips taken out of my wound by the nurse at our local surgery on the 5th. Pat made a special journey from Brockworth on Saturday the 6th to see that her old dad was alive and kicking which was very good of her. On 22nd May it was off to Queen Mary's at Roehampton to Mr. Fawcett's clinic for what I thought was going to be a final check-up, but no. The scan which I had already had showed a slight abnormality on my pancreas which they wanted to keep an eye on which meant another scan after a while to make sure there was no increased growth in the pancreas. We really felt this was care and attention beyond the call of duty and so full marks again to the NHS.

After that life went on more or less as usual and by early June I felt well enough to take a short holiday, which Jean was also more than ready for, which we spent at the Birling Gap Hotel at, would you believe, Birling Gap, high above the white cliffs of the South coast just west of Beachy Head and Eastbourne.

The hotel was not quite as inspiring as its web site had led us to believe and after a very ordinary evening meal on our first night we dined out thereafter!!! It was a nice change and we came home on John's birthday so took Anne and him out for an evening meal which we all enjoyed.

My niece Ann from American with her husband Jim came to England for a flying visit and we were able to see them at John's over a lovely al fresco evening meal.

Queen Caroline, wife of George Third, was bequeathed a palace in the grounds of Kew Gardens which, with the help of lottery funding, had been renovated so at the end of June Jean and I had a day at Kew Gardens which included a tour of the palace. Quite small rooms but very interesting. This was shortly followed by a two day stay at Brockworth for further TLC and recuperation by Pat and Phil. At the end of July Pat and family had a holiday in France so we looked after their two dogs for just over a fortnight, something we always enjoy, particularly if the weather is clement for walking.

On Saturday, September 9th, I paid a visit to Kingston Crown Court which was having an open day for the public. I found it most interesting and it took me back to my magisterial days. I was roped in to be a juror in a mock trial which again took me back to my days in Bishop Auckland where I was a juror at Durham Crown Court over a few days.

After a visit to Mr. Fawcett's clinic at Roehampton on 11th September when all appeared to be going according to plan, we set off on the following day for our fortnight's holiday in and around the north of England. We spent the first two nights with our good friends Brian and Ann Dancer at Ashley in Leicestershire who are very good company, have a lovely newish bungalow, and eat well. We spent one day rambling around Foxton locks on the Grand Union Canal, a flight of 10 locks which were in constant use with narrow boats going both up and down with space in the middle for them to pass.

Our next B&B was at a farm house at Patrick Brompton near Bedale in Yorkshire from where we toured the familiar country of those lovely Yorkshire dales. A picnic by the banks of Semmer Water; a drive over the Buttertubs Pass; a walk on Leyburn Shawl; and a visit to our old friends Betty and Arthur Wise in Richmond after which we toured the remains of Richmond Castle and had a picnic in its gardens.

Our next three nights were spent at Rosedale Abbey, a small village in the heart of the North Yorkshire moors from where we visited Whitby amongst other remembered places.

From there we headed further north towards the main aim of our trip which was to visit the Duchess of Northumberland's garden at Alnwick. Our B&B this time was a farm near Alnmouth, just a few miles from Alnwick, and it was unusual in that all the residents sat round one large breakfast table.

Inevitably there was one person who tended to dominate the conversation; I seem to recall he was a choirmaster or something to do with music which was not everybody's cup of tea. Sorry about the breakfast pun.

The outstanding feature of the Duchess's garden was the cascade of fountains run by a computerised system installed beneath it. Apart from that the garden was separated into various sections including even a poisonous garden which visitors had to be escorted around. It was well worth the journey to enjoy so many different facets of garden design.

On our last day there we had decided to drive up the coast to Bamburgh but the day dawned with a heavy mist so we went inland and drove to Cragside, a N.T, property, once the home of Richard Armstrong a Tyneside ship builder and munitions manufacturer who had used his great wealth and engineering expertise to have the first house lit by electricity and several other innovations. Unfortunately the house was closed for, would you believe, electrical rewiring, so we had to content ourselves with viewing the gardens, lakes, and country drive during which we had our picnic lunch. We did drive on to Bamburgh as the mist had rolled away so we had our coast drive on our way back to our B&B.

My final ultrasound scan was at the beginning of October and it was this test which gave me the all clear on my pancreas.

Our local branch of the N.T. runs outings to various places so, on 12th October, we joined one of these to visit the modern Guildhall Art Gallery followed by a conducted tour of the Mansion House, the Lord Mayor's official residence. Both were interesting and worth seeing.

Towards the end of August we journeyed to Swindon to stay with Sarah and Paul overnight, the object of the visit being to attend a concert given by the Swindon Wind Orchestra which Sarah plays in. There was some rousing music which we, and everybody else, seemed to enjoy.

Our 58th Wedding Anniversary was celebrated on 27th October with John and Anne at our favourite restaurant the Vecchia Roma near Hampton Court.

At the end of November we had a visit from Susi. the lady doctor from Austria with whom we had stayed previously. She was a great friend of Derek with whom she and her late husband had worked out in Zambia. She was a very early riser which disconcerted us a little, taking herself off for a walk at about 6 a.m. We took her on the London Eye then went by taxi to Harrods which she had wanted to visit but with Christmas just four weeks away it was pretty hectic and we were all soon glad to get out of it after a snack lunch and a brief visit to the food hall. We took her to sample the delights of the Vecchia Roma restaurant along with John and Anne. Anne organized a surprise for Jean whose birthday it was the following day by arranging for her sweet course to be delivered with a large sparkler shooting sparks into the air while the lights were lowered and "Happy Birthday" was played over the speakers.

The 4th of December saw me having my annual echocardiogram, for my faulty heart valves, in the morning at Kingston hospital and what I had hoped was to be my final visit to my bowel consultant in the afternoon at Roehampton in the afternoon. I was sure it was time for me to be written off as a bowel patient but Mr. Fawcett surprised me by saying they kept an eye on their patients for up to 5 years so I have many more visits to see that very nice man who has given me a life that I might otherwise not have had.

The usual round of Christmas visits and festivities brought to an end a pretty momentous year which had seen me emerge from darkness to light. It was so good to be alive to welcome our good neighbours for a Christmas meal on 20th December; then John, Anne, Emma and her new love, Mark, for dinner on 21st December: then head off to Brockworth on the 23rd to spend a few nights with Phil's mother who had recently moved into the bungalow next door to her son and daughter-in-law and to enjoy, as ever, the wonderful hospitality of the Hartwells over Christmas.

The year's activities were not quite over for on 27th December Sarah and Paul came for the night to leave their car with us before we took them to Heathrow early, very early, on the 28th for a skiing holiday in France.

We saw the New Year in with our good friends Betty and Cecil across the road from us – and so began 2007 with yet another trip to Heathrow on January 7th to collect Sarah and Paul from their skiing holiday.

Our year's supply of marmalade was made on 9th January.

On a very sad note we received a telephone call on 17th January from the office at Sunset Homes where Derek lived to tell us he had been found unconscious on the floor of his flat that afternoon, having had a fall during the night, and had been taken by ambulance to Guildford hospital. We raced down to Merrow to try and find out more details and then on to the hospital to find Derek in A & E having various tests. We heard later he had been transferred to a ward where we visited him daily but he never recovered consciousness and eventually he died early on the morning of Saturday 20th January. There was, inevitably, a lot to do both in making the funeral arrangements and clearing Derek's rented flat for which we had wonderful help from all our family. It was wonderful to have their loving and practical support at this rather sad time. Everyone, from the Registrar of Births and Deaths to the Funeral directors and the Cathedral authorities were so kind and helpful as we moved towards the day of Derek's cremation on 30th January. A family only service was held at Guildford Crematorium followed by a Memorial Service held in the Lady Chapel of the Cathedral conducted beautifully by Canon Angela and during which Pat spoke about Derek's life as she had known it. She did splendidly and all our children and grandchildren were there to hear her. After the service we had invited those present to join us for refreshments in the refectory so we met many of Derek's colleagues and friends who we had not previously known, and heard things about him from them which we had not previously heard. So, the end of another era with both my brothers now gone which was a strange feeling.

To help us recover from the stress of all the above we booked a few days away at a B&B in Sway, in the New Forest, where we had a quiet time and good food and lodging.

No sooner had we got home but my niece Heather from Detroit along with her husband Jim and son Derek arrived but fortunately Pat and Phil were able to come and meet them and take them to Brockworth for a few days before they descended on us for the rest of their stay. It was rather sad that young Derek had not been able to meet his great uncle after whom he had been named.

Heathrow sometimes seems like our second home. No sooner had we dispatched Heather and family back to the USA than it was the turn of Pat and Phil to come to us to leave their car and be taken to Heathrow for their holiday to South

America while we looked after Benson as usual for 3 weeks. (I forgot to mention earlier that their other dog "Charley" had unfortunately to be put down some time before this.)

I was still undergoing various tests following my colonectomy involving visits to Queen Mary's Hospital at Roehampton as well as continuing my periodical visits to Moorfields Eye Hospital for treatment.

At the end of March the annual production of the Hinchley Manor Operatic Society was "My Fair Lady" which was a really splendid event. They have some very good local talent amongst whom was an exceptional new young Eliza.

Early April saw us on our way to Moseley (Birmingham suburb) where Andrew and Lex live to first of all take them out for an evening meal at a local Italian restaurant and then the following day join them for a tour of Cadbury's World, an Exhibition at the world famous premises of the well known chocolate manufacturer which was good fun. We don't seem to see much of those two so it was good to spend a little time with them.

The John Lewis organization hold an annual event at their country headquarters at Leckford in Hampshire which we visited for the day at the end of May. Lots of interesting stalls and events plus a tractor ride in a trailer round their very extensive fruit, poultry and mushroom farms. After a picnic we took a walk around the attractive water gardens before picking up a bootload of mushroom compost and heading home.

We go "down to earth" occasionally by inviting Gerald and Nick for dinner. Gerald we have known for a long time but Nick is a newer acquaintance, both of them being allotment holders where I used to garden, and they are very good at bringing us garden produce from time to time. Most years I pick enough rhubarb on Gerald's allotment to freeze and last us well into the winter months for rhubarb crumble. They both have good appetites and seem to enjoy their visits to us.

Our annual holiday for 2007 was to the Isle of Man. I used to fly over the island during my short time with the R.A.F. but neither of us had ever been there so it was something

quite new. Having spent the night at Brockworth we set off in the car for Liverpool and the swift (3 ½ hours) catamaran voyage to the island. It was a late crossing so we arrived at our B&B quite late to find "mine host" out on the pavement in pyjamas and dressing gown to welcome us. It had been the island's T.T. motor bike races the previous week so both he and his wife were tired out with having hordes of visitors. He showed us our room and left us to it. During the week the owners went off to the mainland and left us in the care of "minders" whom we liked better than the owners!!! We travelled more or less the length and breadth of the island which has varied scenery and some interesting places such as the Laxey Wheel, and the old House of Keys at Castletown where we re-enacted a session of the old Manx parliament. A super M&S provided us with the wherewithal for lunches and we ate out at various places in the evenings, latterly at the Welbeck Hotel where nearly all the restaurant staff were Polish but very nice and helpful. One oriental waitress whom we seemed to have got to know well actually embraced Jean when she knew we were leaving. An interesting and enjoyable holiday.

On June 2nd with Gerald and Nick (at Gerald's invitation) we drove down to Chestnut Lodge in Cobham to visit the garden there. You would not believe, until you had actually seen them, that in that garden were flamingos, crested cranes, giant carp, a comprehensive aviary, wonderful bonsai trees, tortoises, wallabies and giant lizards. Quite amazing so that a number of our acquaintances whom we told about the garden have also visited on its two annual openings for the National Garden Society.

In August my health had a hiccup when I had rapid heart beats and the doctor told me if it happened again I should call 999. It did happen again 10 days later. I had been rather sick during the night followed by more palpitations so Sarah (who happened to be staying with us) drove Jean and me to Kingston A&E where I was given tests, new medication, and subsequently put on Warfarin to adjust my blood. It was to be another year before the same thing was to happen again.

"Mum" Pat tries to get to stay with us at the time of the Wisley Flower Show (the large one at Hampton Court is now a bit hectic and tiring for oldies) so it was good to have her with us for a few days at the end of August. On this occasion we were able to drive her home by way of Finchampstead where her elder son David and his wife live and although David was away on his work, Pat gave us coffee before we set off again for Brockworth. During our few days stay there we made a visit to Westonbirt Arboretum where there was a most interesting Festival of Wood.

We continue visiting National Trust properties when we can and in September we added Hinton Ampner to our tally.

Emma and I had promised ourselves a visit to the Science Museum for quite a long time and actually made it on 2nd October when we had a happy and interesting day together.

A week later, having joined a local Theatre Club, we made our first outing to see "Fiddler on the Roof" at the Savoy theatre which we felt was somewhat disappointing.

The day after that I was fitted with a 24 hour tape to monitor my heart beat over a full day but I apparently behaved myself for that period.

Shortly after that we paid our first visit to the theatre at Woking where we saw "Car Man", a music and dance show based on the real Carmen and really very good.

Brian and Ann Dancer had kindly invited us to visit them so we had three happy and enjoyable days in their company

On 2nd October we went to Guildford Cathedral for a special service during which the names of those involved with the cathedral who had died in the past year were read out so we heard Derek mentioned.

10th November saw Emma's 30th Birthday party when John and Anne drove us to Brockworth for the day and a few days later we went on our second theatre club outing to the Mill Theatre at Sonning (near Reading) to see a farce, preceded by a 3 course dinner, both of which were enjoyable.

Jean had a nasty fall early in December ripping the skin on her leg so once again we were off to A&E for treatment with a visit to our surgery the following day. Then we went off to Swindon to stay with Sarah and Paul. Jean's leg started to play up again so we spent much of one morning at the Swindon NHS walk-in health centre where an older male nurse treated her very well.

Christmas festivities followed the usual pattern: Christmas meals with both Betty and Cecil then with John and Anne before going to Brockworth for the 25th. We had to come home on the 26th as Andrew and Lexi were going off to Australia on the 27th, leaving their car with us while we drove them to Heathrow.

Another year drew to a close with us having Betty and Cecil for a New Year's Eve dinner followed by champagne at 12 o'clock

As the years move on, and we are now in 2008, our activities seem to concentrate more and more medical and welfare appointments and less and less on recreational outings and holidays as a tedious recital of all our visits to doctors, hospitals, clinics, opticians, podiatrists, etc. would reveal.

Interesting events and activities decline as my age increases and this year in March I will be 86.

Jean had her first cataract operation on 7th January which was a success

Having seen Andy and Lex off to Australia it was now time to get back to Heathrow to collect them on the 16th

Two days later we took the car to Clandon Park to join the West Surrey coach trip to the British Museum to see the Terra Cotta Army exhibition where there was a small but interesting display of some of the warriors and other related artefacts. It was rather crowded but we managed to see what we wanted and it was a worth while day out for us.

22nd January saw us back to Heathrow with Pat and Phil for their holiday in China where amongst many interesting sights they saw hundreds of Terra Cotta Warriors instead of the few we had just seen. We returned to Heathrow in early February to collect the travellers and set them on their way home. It is always something of a relief to get our drive back without other parked cars which make it difficult to get ours parked but we are happy to be able to help the family and other visitors by giving them free parking.

My casual interest in the art of Bonsai took us to Wisley R.H.S. Gardens in February to attend a Bonsai weekend. I love seeing these little old trees of which there were many and varied.

I splashed out and bought a small pink Azalea tree and a new pot for it in which it blossomed beautifully later in the year providing a spot of colour among otherwise small green trees.

A dramatic event occurred on the morning after my 86th birthday when, on March 5th, I followed my usual morning routine to discover, when I got downstairs, that the box in which our car keys were kept was wide open and the keys were missing. On looking outside the front door the car was also missing. I called the police to notify them of the situation and it wasn't too long before a beefy woman police constable arrived to take the details. We cannot be sure how the thief gained entrance to the house but suspect he came in through the garage door. CCTV footage from our next door neighbour's camera showed activity around 1.30 a.m. but the images were too grainy to see much detail. You can imagine our shock and distress at such an unexpected happening. Fortunately we were fast asleep and knew nothing of what had happened but were upset to think someone had been wandering around our house while we were sleeping. The car was found by the police somewhere in London in a state which our insurers treated as a "write-off". In the post a few days after this came a letter from the Metropolitan Police saying they were intending to charge me with speeding on the A3 London road at 2.30 on the morning of the theft so the thief had obviously gone off in haste with the car. I was happily able to prove to the police that I was not the driver on that occasion. We were able to buy a replacement car with the help of money from the insurers and this time we chose an automatic transmission for ease of driving. It took Jean a little time to get used to it but she is now quite happy with it.

Following the theft of the car we had an alarm system installed and a security light fitted but these were rather 'stable door' precautions as such an event is unlikely to happen again.

On 13th March (not a Friday) we joined the coach for the journey to Sonning Mill to see a production of "The Heiress" which we thoroughly enjoyed. This is the outing where dinner is provided before the show and is a really good evening out.

Our friend Jean Stacey came to stay for a few days at the beginning of April and this gave us the opportunity to go out and about with her to one or two places plus an evening meal at a local Italian restaurant which is a treat for us as we don't dine out very often so it is all the more enjoyable when we do.

We were both booked to attend the Tutankhamun Exhibition at the O2 arena in April but Jean was not well so I went with our friend Betty from over the road from us. I found the exhibition a bit disappointing but was very impressed by the O2 arena which seemed so enormous when you were inside it.

At the end of April we took our annual holiday in the Channel Island of Jersey. We drove to Poole where we took the car on the catamaran ferry to St. Helier and then to the rather nice hotel we had chosen for our stay.

It was good to have the car to get about in which made it easy to go where and when we felt like it and to see all we chose to see. It was a most enjoyable holiday except for the night I disgraced myself by having heart palpitations after having got into bed. We phoned the hotel desk who got the hotel manager who called for the ambulance and I was driven off the St. Helier hospital where various tests were done and I was eventually discharged at about 2.30 a.m. The hotel manager had asked us to call him when we were ready to come home and he kindly came for us in his Range Rover. All was well that ended well but at one time I had visions of leaving the island in a box!!!

10th May saw us back at Heathrow to meet second cousin Debi and her friend Janice from Canada. They stayed with us for 6 days which gave us another opportunity to take them out and about including visits to Windsor Castle and the N.T. properties at Clandon Park and Polesdon Lacy.

While they were with us we had another theatre trip. This time to the West End to see "Gone with the Wind" which, since the time we booked the trip, had had pretty poor reviews and we thoroughly endorsed those reviews. The scenery and effects were quite dramatic but it was a disappointing show.

More holiday in June when we had a week's B & B in Devon. Both the places we had chosen turned out to be at the back of beyond but were otherwise comfortable. The first one also did an evening meal and we were happy to dine and wine handsomely with the owners of the place.

Friday 26th September we headed off to Brockworth to spend a night or two to be able to attend the wedding of Emma to Mark. It was a joyous occasion during which we were able to reacquaint ourselves with many of Pat and Phil's old friends who came for the occasion as well as all our own family. Needless to say Pat and Phil made it a wonderfully joyous time. We were very happy to receive Emma and Mark for lunch a few days later before seeing them off at Heathrow for their honeymoon.

The end of October which marked a milestone in our marriage. 27th October brought along our Diamond Wedding which we celebrated well. On Saturday 25th we had a family lunch at a hotel in Kingston when all our family plus a few select friends were present.

During the evening we had many local friends come to the house for drinks and food and at times we had quite a crowd helping us to celebrate the occasion. Most of the family were with us for Sunday lunch on the 26th -. children, grandchildren

and their husbands/wives or friends. John and Anne had given us tickets for the theatre at Richmond which we had not been to for a long time so we enjoyed Oscar Wilde's "An Ideal Husband"

We then had two more trips to Heathrow taking and fetching John and Anne for their holiday to South America.

CHAPTER NINE

As the years roll by our activities become more and more restricted by increasing old age but we are still able to entertain visitors and do trips to and from Heathrow airport when other members of the family were off on their travels. On 1st February, we are now in the year 2009, we had Pat and Phil for a night before taking them to Heathrow the following day. We all awoke on 3rd February to find 4 inches of snow had fallen during the night so the car was to dig out before we could set off, very slowly and carefully, to Heathrow where we left Pat and Phil to meet up with their American friends with whom they were to holiday in India. Later that day we had a phone call from them saying the airport was closing down and there were no flights so, could they please come and spend another night with us. Jean and I hurriedly erected our bunk beds for the two Americans and all four travellers returned from Heathrow by taxi and managed to settle in again for another night. It transpired there were no suitable flights on the following day so it was not until the 4th that they got a taxi to Heathrow and finally were airborne. We had a fun time with the Americans who seemed to enjoy our hospitality.

Emma at this time was living in Peckham and, although it took the best part of an hour to drive over to us, would come and spend a day with us as she did on 15th Feb. when we told her all about the previous week's adventures. We collected Pat and Phil from Heathrow the following day.

At the end of the month Jean managed to fracture her Achilles Tendon and having struggled on with it for a day I decided she must have it seen to so we had a home visit by one of our doctors who confirmed the fracture and arranged an ambulance to A&E at Kingston. I wasn't very well at the time so, very kindly, our friend Betty went with Jean and they were later joined by John whom had been notified of what had happened. Early in the evening Jean arrived home in John's car with an ankle to knee plaster cast on her leg. John produced a wheel chair from his car and a little while later some physiotherapists appeared with all kinds of equipment to help Jean to be comfortable (things to raise a chair seat, a commode, a raised loo seat, crutches, etc.). John brought a single bed down which we installed in the dining room because Jean could not manage the stairs and she spent the next few months living downstairs, washing as best she could in our little downstairs cloakroom, and being wheeled from room to room by me. Pat and Phil came over and Phil and I went to B&Q to get a piece of wood with which he made a ramp so we could get the wheelchair in and out of the front door. For the next 8 or 9 weeks we had a weekly visit to the hospital for Jean's plaster cast to be renewed. When Jean was a lot better she had many weeks of physiotherapy at Molesey hospital and later on at Leatherhead hospital for a few weeks having developed a blood clot in her leg which required special attention.

That was when I started my steep learning curve to do all aspects of housekeeping and cooking for Jean could hardly do anything, having to keep one leg off the floor at all times. We survived with lots of help from family and friends.

It was at this time, in the middle of March, we heard the sad news that my cousin Peter North had died in Japan where he was living.

On 16th June Mikio, the Japanese chap my cousin Peter had been living with, together with his sister and her grown up son came to stay with us for a few days. Mikio could speak a little English but his sister spoke none and her son hardly any so it was a bit difficult at times. It amused us that when we presented a special dish at meal times they would rush for their cameras and take pictures of their meal.

After they had left on the 18th Pat and Phil arrived on the19th to go, I forget just where, bringing little Benson with them. Benson was the little black and white Jack Russell terrier they had had for a long time and who was really on his last little legs when he arrived. He neither ate nor drank and spent the evening lying beside me on the settee until we put him in his basket that night. Jean and I both woke up at about 4 a.m. and crept downstairs to see if he was still alive. He was just breathing so we went back to bed. Pat and Phil arrived back with us on the 20th and, having seen, and heard, what he had been like, rang their vet to be at Brockworth when they got home to have poor Benson put to sleep

He was a great favourite of mine and it was a sad day for us all.

Our only holiday that year was in September when we went to Derbyshire with the main intention of visiting Chatsworth House. We settled on a B&B in the village of

Pilsley outside Bakewell and found it to be a small cottage attached to the post office and our hostess was postmistress as well as doing B&B. We had a good tour of Chatsworth which is a really splendid stately home with extensive and interesting gardens and grounds. From Pilsley we moved on to a farmhouse B&B in Riber. I remember we had some difficulty in finding a decent place to have our evening meal and finished up in a pub with typical pub grub.

For some strange reason which I am at a loss to understand there are no further entries in my diary for the rest of that year so the autumn of 2009 must for ever remain a mystery.

My 2010 diary includes data for December 2009 which shows I was troubled with a urinary infection for the first week of December but after that it is all social or medical dates until 23rd when we went, as usual, to Brockworth for a jolly family Christmas celebration.

On 24th February our very good friend Jean Stacey came to stay for a few days and one of the things we did was to visit the R.H.S. gardens at nearby Wisley, and another was to dine out at our favourite haunt, the Vecchia Roma in Molesey.

Friday 12th March was a red letter day as it was on that day that our first great grandchild was born. Emma gave birth to a fair haired little boy whom they named Noah. What rejoicing there was in the family at this wonderful happening..

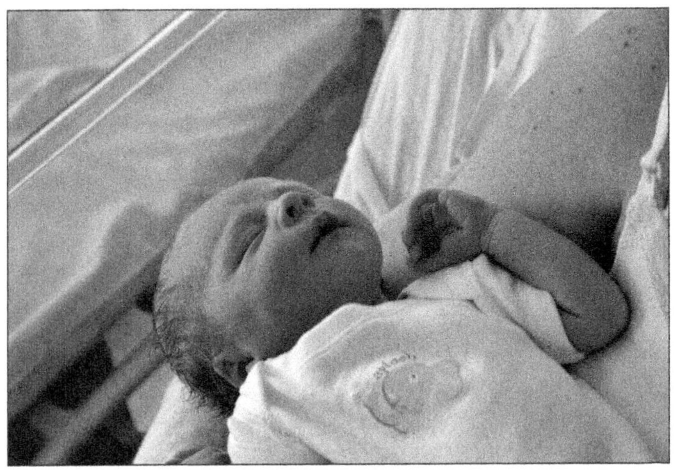

Our daughter Pat reached a milestone on 11th April when she reached her 60th birthday. Of course we had a party and a great celebration.

One of my unfulfilled ambitions was to visit Norwich so, on May 11TH, we set off for that city. We hadn't been too

lucky with our choice of B&B which turned out to be more of a commercial establishment than what we had been used to and it was rather more than the "short walk into the city" than had been advertised. However, I found it an interesting city which we first toured on an open topped bus to get our bearings.

The cathedral with its tall spire was very impressive as were many of the 40 odd medieval churches which the city boasts, many of them now used for other than religious services. One, for instance, housed a puppet theatre. We discovered a lovely little Italian restaurant where the proprietor did all the cooking. Norwich was the only place in my 70+ years of motoring where I collected a motoring offence. I had parked in a car park which I believed to be free after 6 o'clock but turned out not to be. I did appeal but to no avail and came away from the city £40 worse off and with my pride somewhat dented.

At the end of May my niece Ann arrived from America and with her we spent a lovely day at Sheffield Park Gardens which were ablaze with azaleas and rhododendrons. We collected her husband Jim from Heathrow the following day and the day after that they went off to Brockworth to tour the North country with Pat and Phil to explore old family haunts.

On one of our rare days out we visited Eltham Palace in S.E. London. This is an art deco house tacked on to an ancient building. The house has some marvellous marquetry which of course appealed to me. We called in to see Emma and Noah on our way home.

ON 20TH November there was a family gathering at Brockworth on the occasion of Noah's christening. We have a lovely photo of Noah with his mum, Emma, her mum, Pat and Pats mum Jean, the four generations.

The usual Christmas visits ended the year on a high note.

For my 88th birthday in the year 2011 we had a family meal at the Vecchia Roma so it was great to have Pat and Phil and John and Anne to join the celebration. It was on that day that our life style changed for ever as I had decided that, as a result of declining eyesight, I should give up driving. Pat and Phil were able to take the car off our hands and it was sad to see it go but I felt it was the sensible thing to do and we are really very well placed for public transport with a quarter hourly service from the bottom of our road to either Esher or Kingston or Kingston hospital which is very convenient.

Not having a car, it was on 12th March that Paul and Sarah collected us and took us to Peckham to join in the celebrations for Noah's first birthday which was a jolly occasion in a building behind their local pub.

On some of the occasions when Emma and Noah had visited us from Peckham and Jean had perhaps said she couldn't remember certain things Emma told Jean she could get help for her memory loss. Emma, with her psychological knowledge had obviously suspected Jean was having a memory problem. After one or two reminders from Emma we decided to see our doctor so on 20th April we saw Dr. Ingram who gave Jean certain tests after which she referred her to see a psychologist at The Meadows hospital near Epsom.

Life went on as normal until that appointment materialized so, on 29th April along with most of the population of the U.K. we enjoyed the occasion of the wedding of Prince William and Kate Middleton. We attended a memorial service for Trevor Bannister (of Are You Being Served fame) who had died on the shed of his allotment garden while reroofing it. Two days later we had Emma and Noah for lunch and the day after that we had Andrew and Lexi to stay for a couple of days. We made it to Wisley gardens using the local bus services.

On 3rd June we made our first visit to Brockworth using the train. Our good friend Betty drove us to Surbiton where we boarded a train for Waterloo from where we took a taxi to Paddington from where joined a train for Gloucester where Pat was waiting to collect us. We returned by the same method on 7th June.

On 25th June I went to A&E at Kingston having serious diarrhoea. I spent the next 10 days in an isolation ward attached to a drip which accompanied me on my numerous visits to the loo. Hospital food was awful and all the tests I had didn't seem to indicate what had caused the problem but I was so relieved to get out of hospital again after which I got better of my own accord. Pat, bless her, had come to be with mum and look after her while I was not there.

We had previously booked a coach tour holiday with Shearings so, 18th July found us at 8.30 waiting for a feeder coach to take us to the motorway service station at the end of the M1 where we were shunted into a large hall to wait for our transfer to the coach which would take us to our destination in Staffordshire. The hotel was fine and meals were alright. One of the outings was to Trentham Gardens where there was also a monkey forest where I took lots of pictures. There was no excursion for the following day so we took ourselves off on a local bus to Stafford where we had never been.

On Sunday 31st July on the occasion of our gardening friend Gerald's (69th I think) birthday his good friend Nick had arranged a party for him at his allotment shed. Nick had erected a sizeable shelter for some dozen guests under which we enjoyed drinks, sandwiches, cakes, cups of tea and other goodies which he had either prepared or bought. A surgeon's wife (an ex magistrate friend of ours) had made a beautiful sherry trifle and, all in all, it was a really wonderful occasion around a humble allotment shed.

As part of the investigation into Jean's condition we went to Epsom hospital for an MRI scan on her head from which we later learnt she had both Alzheimer's and vascular dementia. Not only had the scan upset Jean but it must also have upset me for, waiting at the bus stop opposite the hospital for a bus to Epsom and thence to Kingston, I felt faint and to avoid doing so sat down on the pavement at the bus stop. Of those other folk waiting for the bus, one took out her mobile phone and was phoning for an ambulance, and an

Indian lady waved a scented thing under my nose. I soon recovered and we went on our merry way.

On 1st September we took the train to Swindon where we were met by Paul who drove us to Purton where we spent a night with Sarah and him before they drove us to Birmingham to be present at the wedding of grandson Andrew to his long time girl friend Lexi. We assembled at Andrew's house where Lexi had hidden herself upstairs to maintain the old tradition of the groom not seeing the bride before the ceremony. The wedding party drove to the Registry Office where a semi traditional wedding took place with Lexi's father arming her in and handing her over to Andrew.

The two mums were witnesses and we were all soon out in a courtyard at the back of the building taking lots of photos. We then drove a little way to a park in the jewellery district of Birmingham for more official photos following which we walked a short way to an Indian restaurant where Lexi's mum had invited the guests for an interesting, (unusual for us) appetizing Indian style meal. In the evening there was a noisy shindig in a room above a pub in Moseley and we eventually spent the night in a B&B before going back to Brockworth the following morning. It was good to see Andrew and Lexi officially man and wife after a long time as 'partners'.

In mid September we took ourselves off by train for a short holiday in the ancient and interesting city of York. My internet choice of hotel turned out not to have been the best one for we had a rather pokey little room and there was no lounge in which to take our ease. Although we knew the city well we took an open top bus tour which showed us some places we had not previously seen. We enjoyed the wonders of the glorious minster and did the museums, including of course the wonderful railway museum, and had tea at Betty's which all visitors should do. An interesting but rather tiring holiday for older people.

On October 26th Beatrix Patricia Hartwell, our second great grandchild, was born in Birmingham to Andrew and Lexi. Lexi is a runner. She does regular training which was preparing her to undertake the Sahara Marathon, a real test of endurance and guts. She had collected the large sum required to enter the race when. to her dismay, just before the race she discovered she was pregnant. She was warned that if she ran the race she might lose the baby but decided to go ahead and run the race she did. It turned out to be much more gruelling than she had expected but she did complete the marathon and the baby completed it as well so all was well. As you will see she had an early outing following her birth.

On 12th November we had a visit from Donna Foster, the local Alzheimer's nurse who gave us lots of information, mainly for me as I had been designated Jean's official carer.

Friday 25th November was a real red letter day for it was on that day that Jean reached the age of 90 and the family duly gathered round to help us celebrate a very special occasion. A party had been arranged to be held in Claygate Village Hall on the 27th when all our family (including 1 month old Beatrix) and a goodly number of friends from far and wide assembled to enjoy catering by Pat and Phil for the food and John and Anne for the drinks while Jean and I toured the hall chatting to everyone. It was a great occasion.

The train journey to Gloucester was becoming more than we could happily manage so it was kind of John and Anne to drive us down to Brockworth for the usual and always very enjoyable Christmas jollifications. Our good friends Betty and Cecil joined us for dinner on 31st December and so ended another momentous year in peace and harmony along with champagne and Christmas cake (the first one I had ever made!!!)

My handwriting is getting to be so much of a scrawl that I am beginning to find difficulty in deciphering some of my diary entries for the year 2012 but we will do the best I can to fill in the closing stages of our lives. Thursday 23rd February at 1.30 at the Day Centre in Claygate saw me attending the first of a 9 week course of meetings for carers addressed by various speakers on the subject of Dementia Awareness. Jean's condition was at this time quite mild and I was horrified and alarmed at some of the stories which other carers told of their various experiences. The meetings gave me an insight into what might lie ahead for us both.

We happened to be at Brockworth on 4th March, my birthday, so I had a family party with Pat and Phil et al.

Jean's annual visit to the Meadows psychiatric hospital near Epsom was on 26th March when she was seen by a charming young black psychiatrist who took her through the usual tests. Unfortunately, her marks out of a possible 30, are going down with each visit showing a slow deterioration in her dementia. This does not in any way diminish her interest in and her care for our house where she regularly does the dusting and the cleaning so it is really only the cooking which I have to do which, although I say it myself, I am becoming quite good at.

Another major event occurred on 12th May with the arrival of Elliot and Lyra, Emma and Mark's twin babies and thus our third and fourth great Grandchildren.

John and Anne were able to drive us down to Emma's house in Churchdown on 2nd June so the twins were just 3 weeks old when we saw them.

This was the time of our great Queen's Diamond Jubilee for which some of the ladies of Manor Drive had initiated a Street Party which took place on Monday 4th June and was a great success.

Jean along with a friend from nearby, being the oldest residents, were invited to open the affair which included three bouncy castles, a cake competition, a crown competition,

children's races, etc. It was only a pity it was such a cold day although many of us were able to remain outdoors to eat our refreshments.

Early in June I had my regular visit to my heart doctor at Kingston hospital where he arranged for me to wear a 24 hour monitor and to have an ECG examination, both of which I did in due course. The results come later.

We had pre-booked a holiday in connection with the R.H.S. of which Jean is a member so early on Monday 16th July saw us waiting at Kingston bus station for our coach to take us to our hotel in Salford, Manchester. The coach was half an hour late which was not a very good start to a holiday but we eventually arrived at a rather nice modern hotel on the quayside of Salford Quays which was the end of the old Manchester ship canal where quite large vessels would sail right up to Manchester. Being a garden holiday we first went to a botanic garden, where we had a tour by a botanist. We also had some time in Tatton Park gardens and later went to the R.H.S. Tatton Park Flower Show. As there was quite a lot of walking it was a tiring holiday but we enjoyed our stay in a nice hotel with good food.

My return visit to Dr. Culling on 12th September revealed that my heart was now fibrillating continuously although there is apparently no way of dealing with that. The doctor said he would write to our doctor recommending more medication but that is still in the pipeline.

Our friend Jean Stacy visited us for a few days at the end of September and as she has a car we were able to enjoy a visit to the R.H.S. gardens at Wisley.

CHAPTER TEN

We come now to 2013 which brought another big change to our lives as you will see.

Towards the end of our Christmas stay at Brockworth we were delighted the discussion got round to the future of the bungalow next door to Pat and Phil.-the bungalow which Phil's mother, Mum Pat as we used to call her, had lived in for 7 years since she moved to it after leaving her home in Oxford. For a number of years I had been anxious to move to Brockworth where we would be close to our daughter in our increasing old age. We had actually looked at one or two properties prior to this but were glad we had

not moved elsewhere because the bungalow was so ideal. The family agreed that it would be ideal for us to move from Hinchey Wood into the bungalow.

Most, if not all, of my readers will have experienced the trauma of moving house and all that that entails. As soon as we got back to Hinchley Wood we contacted an independent estate agent whom we knew who also soon got busy advertising the property. We were staggered at the price the agent put on the house which we had bought for quite a modest sum 37 years previously but, as the price of the bungalow was considerably less than we were hoping to make on our house meant we would have a welcome sum of money to see us through our old age. Everything really worked out for the best in all respects and I felt we were so very lucky. All these things take time and there were so many things to think of – engaging a solicitor, finding a removal firm, informing electric, gas and water suppliers and the like. Unfortunately Jean was not as enthusiastic about the move as I was because she was upset about leaving all the good friends we had made over 37 years in Hinchley Wood. Rather than have prospective purchasers come to view the house individually the agent organised what he referred to as a house sale which was to be held on Saturday 19th January which dawned with quite a covering of snow. Our house was obviously in strong demand for we were told that no less than 22 prospective buyers were going to view the house at 15 minute intervals. We were asked to make ourselves scarce so sought an invitation from our good friends straight across the road from our house so we were able to watch the comings and goings. Several people had made offers on the spot but in the end it was down to two purchasers who had offered the asking price. It ended with blind bids being made by the two parties and we were delighted to lean that a young couple became the new owners of 19 Manor Drive which had served us so well for so long a time.

Our daily life went on as usual while all this was going on with surgery and hospital visits etc. but we were also busy deciding what we needed to take from a three bedroom semi-detached house to a two bedroom bungalow. While we were working hard at our end Pat and Phil were working just as hard to clear and clean the bungalow and redecorate where they thought necessary. Carpets and curtains were already there and all this preparation by Pat and Phil made it was easy to move into a nice clean bungalow.

On the Sunday before moving day we had invited all our friends for farewell party and were pleased that so many of them were able to come and wish us farewell and God-speed to our new home. I could not be sad for I was quite sure we were doing the right thing by moving to where our family were. It meant we were moving away from where John and his wife lived but they were never regular visitors anyway, having their own large set of friends.

The removal men were very good, only missing one small cupboard in which were all our cooking pans so we had to borrow some from Pat until ours had been recovered and delivered to us.

Tuesday 26th March was moving day when all went well and it was not very long before, with the help of Pat and Phil, we were well established in our new home and a new phase in our life began.

Because of her increasing dementia Jean took longer to settle in her new situation and she often bewailed the loss of all her friends in Hinchey Wood but because we didn't know how her mind was working she possibly never got over that loss. It was now, of course, more difficult for her to make new friends.

We very soon registered at the local Brockworth Surgery which is about ½ a mile from the bungalow which is a walk-able distance for us and I regret to say we have kept them fairly busy with our various medical problems and my regular warfarin tests. The doctors and nurses who have dealt with our problems have all been exceedingly nice and helpful.

The few shops in Brockworth supply most of one's daily needs: a well-stocked Co-op, a pharmacist, a newsagent-cum post office, a fish and chip shop, but there is a much better one in the nearby village of Hucclecote. The local Anglican Church of St. George's has a very nice lady vicar and a friendly congregation. Its Church Hall is divorced from the Church and stands between us and the aforementioned shops and holds a number of regular Church activities as well as being available for hire for other organisations.

Brockworth is almost mid-way between Gloucester City in one direction and the lovely town of Cheltenham in the other and there is a 10 minute bus service, with stops about a 10 minute walk away, to either place. There is a Marks and Spencer store in both places but, sadly, no Waitrose which we were used to but there is a big Sainsbury's not too far away to which Pat and/or Phil to take us when they go for a weekly "big" shop.

Jean was always very particular about the very strong head of hair which she was blessed with so we were fortunate to find "Jan" from the local hairdresser who would come to the bungalow each week and give Jean a shampoo and set, or a perm when necessary. We therefore had pretty well all we needed for daily living.

The local hospital which we needed to visit quite often was the Gloucestershire Royal Hospital situated on our side of Gloucester City but our bus services nearest stop was a 10 to15 minutes' walk away. Here again Pat and/or Phil were so very good at delivering us there and collecting us later that we have not very often had to use the bus and take the walk. We have been most fortunate in that all the various specialists we have seen, and all the surgeons who have operated on us (more of this anon) have given us high class service. I would not be alive to tell you all this had it not been for the NHS and its staff of nurses, doctors and surgeons.

Our lives settled down to a fairly regular pattern, part of which was an almost daily visit from our lovely daughter Pat with less regular ones from Phil as well as occasional visits from younger granddaughter Emma, initially with her only son Noah, and later with the twins Lyra and Elliot, always such a joy to Jean who now lived largely for her family as the most familiar beings her dementia left to her.

We received an almost weekly invitation to share Sunday lunch next door with Pat and Phil along with various other members of our family who, as I have said, Jean was always delighted to be with. John was very good at driving over from Wimbledon as often as he could and was always very kind and considerate to his Mum. Although Jean would do a little light cleaning it became necessary for us to employ a cleaner and through the agency which Emma recommended us we employed a middle aged lady, Barbara by name, to come for 2 hours every Tuesday afternoon to dust and clean and vacuum and has been coming regularly now for 18 months.

Sunday 28th April was a red letter day for it was the occasion of the Christening of Emma and Mark's twins which took place in the Anglican Church in Churchdown which they all attend. Lyra and Elliot behaved themselves well I seem to remember then we all went back to the Churchdown residence for a large family gathering. Their first birthday was exactly two weeks later on 12th May. Another special occasion occurred a few days later when we were able to invite Pat and Phil to dinner with us prior to them going on holiday. It was so good to repay some of their hospitality for once but it always seems strange when they are not in residence next door.

All this time blood tests, warfarin tests, hairdressing, podiatry, (I could no longer get down to cut my toe nails) etc. were going on apace but it is not necessary to go into any detail about these.

The local Alzheimer's nurse was a young lady called Sam Harris. For her appointment with Jean she turned up at the bungalow on an electric powered bicycle and wrapped in warm clothing, goggles and helmet. She was so lovely with Jean while testing her and just chatting and being friendly. The results of Jean's tests showed a regular decline in her memory but there is no treatment for this decline, one just has to live with it, sadly.

As Jean's carer I had everything to do for her, morning, noon and night and this I had done to the best of my ability for about 4 years with very little respite for myself. To alleviate this a little we arranged for Jean to be taken to a respite home each Thursday afternoon from 12 noon to about 4 p.m. when she was brought home again. This was the only break I had from constant caring and everyday cooking but it was better than nothing and continued from the beginning of May until the end of the year.

At the end of May I had my first of several appointments with the Audio Outpatients Clinic at Gloucester Royal Hospital (GRH henceforth) because I felt I was not hearing all the conversations going on around me. I was given a comprehensive hearing test in each ear and it was decided to fit me with a hearing aid in my left ear which was the worst one. We went off and waited for another appointment to have the device fitted...

In the course of the next 3 weeks we had visits from John and Anne, Joan Brown, a friend from Hinchley Wood, and Jean and Geoff who were previously our next door neighbours in Manor Drive, all of which were welcome diversions for Jean.

On 24th June I was again at the Audio clinic at GRH when I had my hearing aid fitted. This was the model which is moulded to you ear to fit close inside the ear. It seemed to work in some situations but not in others but I persevered with it until such time as I went for a review. Four days later I was at the GRH to attend an eye clinic. In this instance I do not think Gloucester took half as much trouble with my declining eyesight as had Kingston where they checked up on me every three months I have not had a follow up from that day to this but, realistically there is not much they can do to improve or halt the decline in my sight. I have a wish that I die before I go blind. On Thursday 11th July John came to stay a night before taking us off the following morning to spend a few days with him and Anne in Wimbledon. The primary reason behind this visit was to attend the 90th birthday celebrations of our good friend Cecil Fitzwilliam. His younger son Peter and his wife Vivienne had arranged the party at their house in Raines Park which was only a short car ride from John's house. It was a baking hot day so there were sun awnings in the garden under which we had slap up lunch with many of Cecil's friends and family, most of whom we knew. It was quite a party.

I was of the opinion that we might never get to see the sea again so had booked a sea front hotel in Eastbourne for a few days. Apart from breakfast the hotel served no food so for lunch we found a coffee-cum-ice cream parlour further along the front while for our evening meal there was a much larger hotel quite near in the other direction where we ate well. There was by this time a limit to the amount of walking we were able to do so we had to find things to do which didn't involve too much walking. One day we took the hop on hop off bus and got off at a rare breeds sheep farm where we saw sheep shearing and then wool spinning from the same wool. We also had a rather bumpy tractor ride around the farm. On another day we took a bus along the coast to Brighton where there is an aquarium I had long wished to visit and which I enjoyed. Brighton was seething with people so we didn't stay long. We only had three nights at the hotel but it was a very welcome break and possibly our last sight of the sea. Anne came to pick us up for the drive back to Wimbledon and John got us back to Brockworth. At 11 a.m. on Monday 12th August saw me back at the Audio outpatient's clinic as GRH for a review of my hearing aid. They discovered my ear channels were too narrow for the regular type of hearing aid so fitted me up with a different type. Again I persevered with this other one until my next appointment.

We did see the sea again as I had booked a holiday with a Cheltenham firm for a 5 day tour of the Lake District. Our hotel accommodation was pretty poor but at least the food was quite good. The hotel was located right beside the sea at St. Bees Head which was nice but it was quite a long way from any of the Lakes which meant longish periods in the coach before getting near the lakes. This has been the criticism I have had about coach holidays. Unfortunately on the second day Jean had a fall down a few steps and was both wounded and shocked. Paramedics were called and then the ambulance which took us to Whitehaven Hospital for an X-Ray and patching up. Bravely she went on the remaining outings.

The bathroom in the bungalow had a brightish blue suite of bath, wash basin and toilet which I hated and had decided to have them removed and replaced with something a little less gaudy. With Phil's valuable help and advice we chose white fittings as well as a walk in shower instead of the one which was over the bath and difficult for Jean to access. It all worked very well and I am very pleased with my lovely modern bathroom.

Because of Emma not being so well and having the twins to cope with as well as Noah I started supplying them with cakes, biscuits, flapjack etc. and have become quite an accomplished baker. My repertoire includes Victoria Sponge with Raspberry jam or Lemon Curd, Lemon Drizzle, Chocolate, and Sticky Toffee Cake but they seem to like Flap Jack best of all. My Christmas cake had been made sometime previous to this and as Christmas was fast approaching it was time to get it out and be fitted up with almond icing and sugar icing. The cake was quite a success and lasted us well into the New Year. We enjoyed Christmas with the usual Christmas feast shared by most of the family and provided by Pat and Phil and so 2013 passed into history.

There were some big changes in 2014 especially to our way of life. Jean's dementia was slowly getting more difficult for me to deal with. I had cared for her morning, noon and night for 4 or 5 years and was becoming increasingly unable to do what was required for her welfare as well as being concerned about my own welfare. After some consideration of the situation the family agreed that the time had now come for Jean to have better care than I could give her. Fortunately there was just the right place near enough for me to go and visit Jean almost every morning for an hour and a half or so.

On 6th January Millbrook Lodge Care Home became Jean's permanent residence.

She was not at all happy about this for some considerable time and constantly talked about when she could return to the bungalow. There was no problem with visiting so Pat would call in when she was passing or when she had a moment. Occasionally Emma would take the twins in to see their great granny which she really loved. By this time Jean no longer read books, or watched TV. She could hardly carry on a conversation so I think she must have had a lonely life for most of the time. The staff were very caring and considerate and although various activities were arranged for the residents Jean was unable to take part in them. I used to take in a little parcel of chocolate, or biscuits, or fruit and suchlike and on most days she had eaten the lot before it was time for me to leave. Her regular hairdresser, Jan, continued to do Jean's hair in Millbrook Lodge where there was a dedicated hairdressing salon. Jean never did get back to the bungalow or see the new terraced front garden which was being built at that time

The front garden lawn sloped down to a wall beside the public path and was rather difficult for me to mow which

meant another chore for Phil to do. I got quotes from landscape gardeners for what I had planned and they in turn made suggestions. The work was carried out at the worst part of the year which turned out to be also very wet so they had a struggle at times to get on with the job.

I am delighted with the finished work so I now have a lower terrace covered in slate pieces and having 7 shrubs growing merrily which I hope will soon grow large enough to make a show, and an upper terrace mainly laid to lawn but with a small bed along the front for a little colour.

I now had to adjust to living by myself which at first felt very, very strange and took quite a bit of getting used to. I had nearly always organised breakfast but it seemed odd to be sitting at the breakfast table by myself. Jean nearly always made the bed which I now have to do. Lunch again was now a lonely meal and it was now I who had to make sure there was the necessary food in the refrigerator or the freezer for all my meals. Thus all the household activities such as washing, ironing, and cooking now became my responsibility and if I didn't do it, it didn't get done. I had to remember to change the bedding regularly and also the bathroom towels. Fortunately we already had our cleaning lady coming in for two hours each week and that seemed to be adequate to keep the bungalow clean. Not having the best of memories I came to rely very much on my diary in which were written all my doctors and hospital appointments and when to collect my pills from the pharmacy. Also listed in the diary were all the family birthdays and wedding anniversaries so that I should not forget to send cards on the appropriate days. It all seems to be working quite well and it was not long before I fell into the new routine.

At about 2 a.m. on the morning of 14th March, ten days after my 91st birthday, I was woken with a pain across my abdomen. I thought it must have been from something I had eaten the day before so thought little of it until, gradually, the pain got increasingly worse and worse until at about 6 a.m. I could bear it no longer. The alarm system which had been installed for Jean was still active so I called for an ambulance which duly arrived with three paramedics who, after having done their preliminary examination decided I should go to A & E at Gloucester Royal Hospital. I was not really conscious of what went on there because by this time I was barely conscious but I understand that first I was give an E.C.G., followed by an x-ray and then a Scan, all of which confirmed I had a knot or twist in my small intestine. What had caused this I shall never know but I have never known of such an event. Fortunately there was a surgeon, with the unusual and fascinating name of Mr. Dwerryhouse, on hand to perform an emergency operation which saved my life as the alternative to an operation in such a case is an early death. I spent five days in intensive care during which I had frightening hallucinations, followed by two weeks in a small side ward. Following the operation I had to wear an oxygen mask continually. When I was due to be discharged from hospital Pat and Phil were away on holiday so it was my grandson-in-law Paul, (Sarah's husband) who volunteered to prepare the bungalow to receive an invalid and to look after him for a few days. I am unable to express adequately the admiration I have for the expert and understanding way in which Paul cared for me for three days while I readjusted myself to normal life. He was as good as, if not better, than a trained nurse and I can never thank him enough for all that he did for me. The district nurses came regularly for many days to change the dressings on the wound on my stomach.

Since that time my walking seems to have deteriorated and it was not long before I was needing walking aids to get myself about. Instead of going to the surgery for my warfarin test the nurse came to the bungalow to do them. My diary indicated that my first outing since the operation was on 5th May (a Bank Holiday) to a BBQ at Emma and Mark's. Not a very nice day as I recall so most of the eating was done inside rather than out.

Jean had been regularly smitten, and consequently been very uncomfortable with a prolapsed bowel and it was decided she should have an operation to cure this so she now had a spell in hospital.

A blood test revealed I was deficient in Vitamin B12 so I had a series of five injections to try and remedy this deficiency. By this time I had been given a four wheeled walking frame which enabled me to walk to the surgery, a distance of about half a mile. I was able to take the frame on the bus so could still make the journey to either Gloucester or Cheltenham. It was also possible for me to get myself to and from the hospital but, usually Pat or Phil would drive me there and I would make my own way home by bus.

On the evening of Sunday, 24th August I received a telephone call from Millbrook House to say that Jean had been taken to hospital because of her deteriorating condition. I went to the hospital on the Monday morning to find Jean in a 6 bedded ward. She was barely conscious, not able to talk and not taking food. I sat with her for the rest of the day with a short break for food from the hospital shop. The following day followed the same pattern except that Jean was fully unconscious and it was sad to sit there with no response. On the third day, 27th August, I was sitting beside her bed just watching her breathing when, at 2.25 p.m., quietly and peacefully I watched her breathing cease and realised that my dear wife of 65 years had finally left me. I could not be really sad because I knew she was now free from the suffering she had been going through recently but it was a very strange feeling to be without my life time companion.

As the result of the vicar being on holiday it was not until Monday 15th September that we were able to arrange a funeral. On that day family members only gathered at the crematorium at 1.30 for a short service conducted by the vicar, Rev. Jane Walden. I was so moved by her short address as well as by the sadness of the occasion that by the end of the service I was crying copiously. At the close of the service as the coffin slowly disappeared behind the closing curtains I sprang to my feet to bid a final farewell to my dear wife's mortal remains and left the crematorium hardly able to see where I was going. The funeral car took us home for a break and then on to St. George's for a memorial service at 2.30. Although Jean had had hardly enough time to make many friends the church was well filled and included three or four friends who had travelled from Hinchley Wood for the occasion. During the service Pat and John recounted to the congregation some of their memories of their mother: Andrew read a message from Emma who was too ill to attend: and I read a passage before saying a few words of my own about Jean. At this service again the vicar gave a most moving address and once again I was in tears by the time it ended. I remember that during the final hymn I slipped out of my pew into the pew behind where Pat was sitting and hugged her for comfort. We had hired a firm of caterers for the reception which was held in the church hall and where most of the congregation joined the family for an informal time of chatting and reminiscing. This was not quite the end of the matter for, on 25th November which would have been Jean's 93rd birthday a few of the family gathered in the burial ground at St. George's church where we interred Jean's ashes and laid a memorial stone over them. The family have prudently left space for my name to join hers in due course!!!

CHAPTER ELEVEN

Due to Jean's dementia we had not been able to have a real holiday for a few years so I considered treating myself to a cruise. The family seemed to approve this idea so I chose to go on a Saga cruise to the Caribbean. This was due to leave Southampton on 13th January so I had heaps of time to get used to the idea and to gather together an appropriate wardrobe to cover the 5 weeks of the cruise.

All this time my surgery and hospital appointments continued apace. I have regular checks on my Warfarin situation and occasional blood tests from which the doctors can learn a lot about the patient's condition. Hospital visits were to clinics for eyesight, hearing and heart matters and dermatology for my spotty head.

22nd October was a sort of red letter day because I had a visit from Bob and Joy Curzon for tea. I had long been conscious that I had had no visitors with the exception of family members and it was so refreshing to entertain a couple whom I had got to know quite well from church and also a Monday morning church coffee morning. After 20 months in Brockworth they were my first real visitors with the exception of a few Hinchley Wood friends who had journeyed specially to see Jean and me and were quite refreshing. Subsequently Bob has dropped in a couple of times and it is good to have a congenial man to chat to.

Towards the end of November, to give me a little break, John came and took me back to their Wimbledon house for a few days which I really enjoyed. They say it never rains but it pours and such was the case as Sarah and Paul invited me to Purton for the weekend which was also a treat for me.

We are now into December when Christmas began for me with an invitation to a Mother's Union Christmas dinner at a well-known local pub. Pat is a member of this church organisation so was able to include both Phil and me for a very enjoyable evening. The meal was excellent and was followed by the singing of a few carols and a few amusing short speeches. There was a good raffle to which I had donated a bottle of wine and from which I came away with not one but two prizes

I don't know if I have made it clear how very ill Emma had been for quite a long time and the very sad outcome was that just before Christmas the poor girl had to have her right leg amputated just above the knee. It was a brave, but perhaps the only sensible decision on her part but I admired how bravely she came through this drastic operation but, also how much better she looked and seemed, after the operation. I long for the time when she can be fitted with a prosthesis to help her to get about better.

The Hartwell family have for many years held a family reunion and in time gone by there were quite a large collection of them. Gradually, over the years, the numbers have dwindled until now it is only two families and their children who qualify. However, as the odd man out, I was invited to join the 2014 Hartwell family reunion hosted by Sarah and Paul in their house in Purton. This was a lively family gathering with a jolly good feast which I was glad to be able to share with the Hartwells.

I spent most of Christmas Day with my family next door at Pat and Phil's house. With the exception of Andrew and Lexi all the family took part in a scrumptious Christmas dinner and the exchange of presents. It was a real traditional Christmas which I thoroughly enjoyed but I have to say it was something of a relief to take myself back next door to my bungalow as an escape from screaming children who were wanting each other's presents.

I saw in the New Year, 2015, at the home of Linda and Colin, friends of Pat and Phil, who had kindly invited me in their invitation to spend the evening with them.

It is now, as I write, the first week in January 2015. These lines are now being written contemporaneously so it was the day before yesterday when I realised I had a urinary infection. Having had them several times before, I was aware of the symptoms. I took a specimen of urine to the surgery yesterday where the infection was confirmed and a prescription for antibiotics was taken to the pharmacy. These are now being taken to ensure I am free of infection by sailing date next Tuesday.

Yesterday was start date for the last of my major alterations to my bungalow. There was a small conservatory attached to the back of the bungalow with access through doors at the back of the lounge. I decided I would like this enlarged so that it encompassed the back door from the kitchen so that it would be possible for me to go straight out into the conservatory from the kitchen. This would enable me to have my breakfast in the conservatory without having to trail round to the dining area of the lounge. I hope it will be completed by the time I come back from my cruise. The bungalow will then be as I envisaged it when first I knew we were coming to live in Brockworth.

January 13th arrived all too quickly but my bags were packed and waiting when the chauffeur driven car, courtesy of Saga, drove up with two lady passengers already in it and we were soon on our way bound for Southampton and the M.V Saga Pearl II, the smaller of Saga's two ships. I did not have long to wait before I was aboard and exploring a rather small cabin. It had a window, not a porthole, a double bed, a chair and writing desk, cupboards and a bathroom with a small shower. While it had all one really needed for everyday living it was rather too small to spend much time in. I forgot to say it had a TV with only one BBC channel and several ships' channels. I soon set off to explore the ship with its lounges, bars, library, restaurants and shop. I was not interested in their swimming pool. The stewards were all Philippinos who were always cheerful

M/V Saga Pearl II
My rough log of my 35 day cruise on Saga Pearl II

DAY 1. Tuesday, 13th January.

A chauffer driven car collected me and my luggage (2 lady passengers were also in the car) at 10 30 a.m. and dove us to Southampton Ocean Terminal where we boarded the Saga Pearl II at about 2.30 p.m. I was conducted to my cabin and then for an Embarkation Buffet which I was by then more than ready for. Sandwiches and cake but lots more goodies for those who wanted them. Food was to be a feature of the cruise. My cases were delivered to my cabin and I spent some time packing thing away in cupboards and drawers. Obligatory boat drill was at 4.30. Then there came a message from the captain over the tannoy saying there were 20ft. waves in the Bay of Biscay and he had decided to shelter in Cherbourg for the night which we did. And so to bed in my comfortable double bed.

DAY 2. Wednesday 14th January.
Woke at 6.30, raised my window blind to see the lights of Cherbourg through pouring rain and with lightning flashing. A steward brought my breakfast to the cabin on a tray. I took a shower in the tiny cubicle about 1 metre by ½ metre and dried myself on a bath sheet almost as big as the bathroom. (We had clean towels and face cloth every day). Lovely tender rack of lamb for dinner. The evening entertainment was a lady singing a lot of Karen Carpenter songs. I didn't like her voice but the music was good.

DAY 3. Thursday, 15th January.
Departed Cherbourg at 11 a.m. By 4 p.m. we were in the open sea heading into the Bay of Biscay where the ship pitched and rolled in a heavy swell. During the day I met a pleasant Welshman and his wife and also another passenger who had joined the Royal Navy a year later than me. Discovered there were more women passengers than men and that some 90% of the passengers were regular cruisers. Went to my bunk early, missing the evening entertainment by a magician. Woke at 10.30 to the sound of crashing and banging as the ship was being thrown about wildly.

DAY 4. Friday 16th January.
I woke at 7 a.m.in time to receive my breakfast tray at 7.30. I was up and about by 10 a.m. in time to attend a lecture about the "Tall Ships" followed by a lazy lounge in the library until lunch time. At the lunch table I met a nice man whose nick name was 1/6d (his real name was Bob Tanner). After lunch I went with them to form a team for a quiz which we won..

DAY 5. Saturday, 17th January.

I woke to a dark, grey morning with a big swell still running giving the ship some lively movements. Discovered my i.pad could not sent emails so phoned Pat to tell her not to expect messages. Had another lazy day.

DAY 6. Sunday, 18th January.

There was a nondenominational church service this morning which I attended. The service was conducted by the ship's chaplain, Archdeacon Arthur Hawes. The service was followed by communion but as the ship was rolling we stayed in our seats and the communion was brought round to the communicants. In the evening I attended a talk about Faberge and his famous eggs.

Today was the first of several occasions when we had to turn our clocks and watches back by one hour.

DAY 7. Monday, 19th January.

Although I sleep well on my double bed I woke at 6 a.m. I pulled up my window blind and saw the lights of Ponta Delgada, capital of the Portuguese Azores. The ship was soon berthed alongside a quay, the gangway lowered and the port officials came on board and cleared the ship so that the passengers could go ashore. I had previously booked a place on a panoramic bus tour of the island so joined a coach for this trip. Our first stop was at the lip of an extinct volcano crater some 13 miles round, with a lake and a village at its base. Ponta Delgada is a pretty city with houses painted all colours set in narrow streets. We returned to the ship in time for lunch. Because of the weather the outer decks had been closed to passengers so this afternoon I took the opportunity to inspect the various outer decks. Sailed from the Azores later in the day for 6 more days at sea before reaching the Caribbean Islands..

DAY 8. Tuesday, 20th January.

All around us today is the wide, wide ocean over which at lunchtime a little strong sun shone but it was mainly cloudy.

I went into the lounge at 4.15 for afternoon tea and was invited to be with my Welsh friend Ron and his wife Joyce Suddenly the Captain appeared and joined us for quite a long chat. Although he is a Dutchman about 6'4 or 5' he has Welsh connections so got on well with Ron. Today was one of several formal days when the gentlemen dressed in evening dress for dinner and the ladies put on their finery. I went to the evening concert but it was not my style so I walked out after the first song and went to my bunk.

DAY 9. Wednesday 21st January.

I had put my name down for a visit to the ship's navigating bridge and today a number of us visited holy territory. 70 years had made enormous changes to the way ships are now navigated across the empty seas. There is now GPS, a satellite which gives the ship's position to within a few yards. 70 years ago the ship's position was fixed at noon with a sextant and mathematical workings. Few ships had radar 70 years ago but now all but a few do have it. This screen shows the area around the ship and any other vessels that may be in the area. So much mechanical equipment replaced the human eyes. Very little was as I remember it in my M.N. days.

I had a session with the new computer guru who assured me that the Emails I thought I had sent from my iPad had not been delivered but he kindly sent them on one of the ship's computers.

Tonight was formal dressing up night again and again I walked out of the evening entertainment as being not my style.

DAY 10. Thursday 22nd January.

For some reason I woke at 5.30 but when I raised my window blind it was to see a bright and clear blue sky. At 12 noon I joined some 70 other "singles" for a special lunch to try and help us to get to know each other. After each course two of us moved to another table and another set of names. I don't think I was able to remember any of the names. At dinner that evening I listened to all my fellow diners who were dedicated and regular cruisers discuss their experiences on the various cruise ships they had travelled on. The evening entertainment had to do without my presence again.

DAY 11. Friday 23rd January.
Rather cloudy today but quite warm when out of the wind. Spent quite a long time doing my favourite thing, sitting in an easy chair and watching the sea roll by before going up to the Veranda restaurant to make myself a coffee. This I took out on deck and watched the Philippino waiters setting up a fish and chip stall for a fish and chip lunch. Saw a lovely rainbow astern. I then went to the very top public deck which gave the opportunity for a good walk which took one past the tennis court and with a good view of the foredeck which one otherwise never saw.

The gentleman beside me at dinner tuned out to be a retired London "Cabbie" who had been on several cruises including one round the world cruise.

DAY 12. Saturday 24th January.
Misread the time on my clock and ended up showered and shaved by 5,45 a.m. Went up to the Veranda restaurant for an early cup of coffee Spent some time out on deck in lovely warm sunshine.. Nothing very exciting to report. The early part of the evening entertainment was given by a quartet of young string musicians who played some Viennese music which I enjoyed. But not the cabaret following which I walked out of.

DAY 13. Sunday 25th January.
I was up to the toilet several times in the night so took a urine specimen to the ship's sick bay where they confirmed I had a urinary infection for which I was given antibiotics.

I attended the interdenominational Church service and took communion after the service.

I see I have noted that I had good dinner companions this night which was rather unusual.

Spotted a few flying fish which I hadn't seen for 70 years.

Tonight is Burn's Night and the Captain and his officers are holding a cocktail party to mark the occasion. I then had my first taste of Haggis in a meat ball.

DAY 14. Monday 26th January.

Whilst eating my breakfast I noted a few birds flying alongside the ship giving an indication that we were not very far from land. Spent some time up on deck basking in glorious sunshine. A very lazy day until evening when the young string quartet gave another very good concert.

DAY 15 Tuesday, 27th January.

Scarborough, Tobago.

When I looked out of my cabin window at 6 a.m. expecting to see a lovely tropical island I was met with a low strip of grey land under leaden skies. After an early breakfast the sun did begin to shine and turned the day into another hot sunny one. By 8.30 a.m. the ship was alongside the quay and the gangway had been lowered. I went ashore with a lot of other passengers to join coaches for a panoramic tour of the island. Our first stop was at Fort St. George (built by the British to repel the French) then to other locations, ending up at a humming bird farm.

During our tour of the most easterly of the Caribbean islands the procedure was for the ship to arrive at the island in the early mornings then leaving at about 5.30 in the afternoon for an early morning arrival at the next island. We only had one day on each island.

DAY 16. Wednesday, 28th January.

St. George's, Granada

Stayed on the ship this morning and visited the launderette where I washed some of my things and ironed three shirts.

Had a little walk into the town after lunch. Once across the road and past the first row of houses and shops the streets climbed steeply. The place seemed rather untidy but many of the buildings were painted in different colours.

The Fred Olsen cruise ship "Braemar" was on the other side of the quay.

Day 17. Thursday 29th January.

Hillsborough, Carriaccou.

I felt sick through the night and was eventually sick at about 4 a.m. but retained my stomach pains. I had pre-booked a shore excursion so handed my ticket in so another passenger could take my place, I spent a miserable day in my cabin without any food. All I saw of this island is what I could see out of my cabin window.

DAY 18. Friday, 30th January.

Kingston, St. Vincent

The ship anchored off shore early this morning. As I had been sick a second time I decided it was time to go and see the ship's doctor again which I did. Following his examination and questioning he said I must stay in my cabin for fear of transmitting my problems to other passengers. My food was thin consommé soup. I hadn't come on a cruise to be shut in my cabin!!!

DAY 19. Saturday 31st January.

Bridgetown, Barbados

From my cabin window I saw that the ship docked at about 7.30 and the gangway was lowered right outside my cabin window so a little later I was able to watch lucky passengers going ashore, I had an excursion ticket for Bridgetown and was bemoaning my fate when a phone call from a nurse told me I was now out of quarantine. I hurriedly put on some clothes and was all ready to join my excursion when another all from the sick bay told me I must remain in quarantine. So much for Barbados where I had especially wanted to go ashore.

DAY 20. Sunday, 1st February

Roseay, Dominica

The ship was alongside the quay in good time and before long the gangway was in place and passengers were going ashore, but not me. From what I saw from my cabin window it looked a rather mountainous island.

Day 21 Monday 2nd February.

Little Bay, Montserrat

The ship anchored off-shore at about 7 a.m. and passengers were going ashore in the ship's tender about an hour later. The sky is very cloudy and overcast and the mountains on this rather forbidding looking island are covered in cloud. "Summer in the Caribbean!!!"

DAY 22. Tuesday, 3rd February.

Blowing Point, Anguila

My scribbled log is very sketchy and seems to suggest I was able to go for breakfast today but had to rush to the loo in the middle of it with diarrhoea. Off to the doctor again who gave me Imodium and an orange drink and sent me off to stay in my cabin all day.

DAY 23. Wednesday, 4th February.

St. John, Antigua

This was the day I should have taken my helicopter ride over Montserrat but as I still felt unwell I went to the doctor who decided I should not take the trip. So fed up I didn't even bother to take any photos of the island. Took lunch in my cabin but rallied to have a small dinner in the dining room.

DAY 24. Thursday, 5th February.

On this day we set sail for Madeira and we spent this and the next five days at sea.

DAY 30 Thursday, 12th February.

Funchal. Madeira

Rose and showered by 7 a.m. for an early breakfast before joining my shore excursion. This was a tour of Funchal and surroundings in a long wheelbase, rather old, Land Rover in which 5 of us rattled up hill and down dale around Funchal. There were some very steep little roads (1 in 4 or less) and some hairpin bends as well as a couple of times the driver went off road on very rough forest tracks. We stopped several times in interesting locations. Funchal is built on the side of a fairly steep hill.

Day 31 Friday 13th February.
At sea bound for Lisbon.

Day 32 Saturday 14th February,
Lisbon, Portugal.

Woke at 7.30 to find the ship alongside the quay and the gangway being lowered right in front of my cabin window. After breakfast went ashore, got the shuttlebus into the city and then took a ride on an open top red city tour bus which gave me a good idea of what the city was like. I rated it as a fine city from what I saw with some good open spaces, squares, gardens etc. The weather was rather cold and miserable. In the afternoon had more episodes of diarrhoea so went to see the doctor who gave me Imodium and once again put me in quarantine in my cabin. So once again I was back on consommé soup and shut away from the crowds.

Day 33 Sunday 15th February.
At sea in the bay of Biscay bound for Southampton.

DAY 34 Monday 16th February.
At sea and it was not quite as rough as yesterday.

DAY 35. Tuesday 17th February.
Woke early this morning after a very unsettled night to find the ship gliding up the Solent on its way to its final berth at

Southampton Ocean Terminal. I had to be out of my cabin by 8 a.m. but was not due to go ashore until 9.45 so spent some time getting some breakfast, like so many other passengers, but was glad when it was my turn to go ashore and join the car which took me home.

It had been an interesting experience but the enjoyment of the cruise had been rather marred by my catching various bugs and missing out on quite a lot of what I should have joined in. I do not think I will be ocean cruising again.

In spite of the rather bad experience I had on my first cruise (I was wont to tell other passengers I had done plenty of cruising 60 years earlier during the second world war) I nevertheless chose to go cruising again in July of that year. This time it was on Saga's larger ship, The M.V. Sapphire had larger cabins than the Saga Pearl II and was altogether roomier with spacious public rooms and restaurants. The ship sailed to the western Mediterranean and called at Italian, Spanish and Portuguese ports only one of which I had previously been to.

Now, in October 2015, I have booked a Saga River Cruise in May 2016 down the Rhine from Switzerland and into the Danube as far as Budapest.

EPILOGUE

"Nothing goes on forever" goes the old saying and those words must apply to this life story of mine if it is ever to be produced in book form which has been the object of the exercise so that future generations may have the opportunity of finding out what life was like in the 20th and early 21st centuries for the average man. I now regret not asking my parents about their early lives and I would advise my readers to do this before it is too late.

Mine has been a good life which I have always (well, nearly always) tried to live by the Christian principles which were taught to me by my mother. So you see how one generation has an impact on another generation and I hope that some of the aspects of the life portrayed in this book may be adopted by whoever may read it. You only have one life, do the best with it that you can.

ADDENDUM

(Here is space for any notes you may wish to make)

Lightning Source UK Ltd.
Milton Keynes UK
UKOW07n1658060117
291553UK00001B/1/P

9 781781 489864